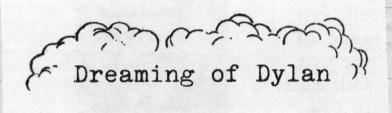

Dreaming of Dylan

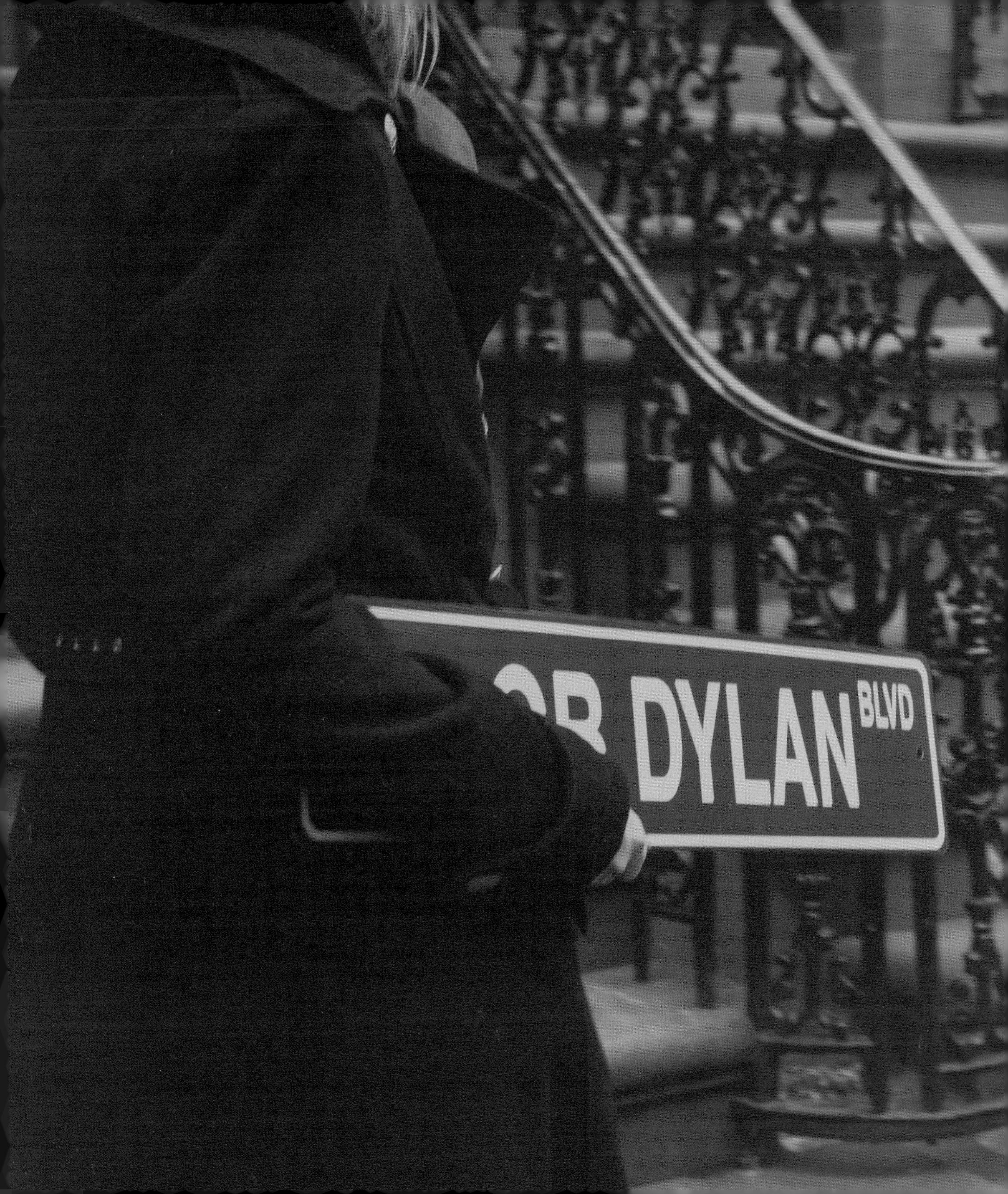
DYLAN BLVD

DREAMING

OF

DYLAN

115 Dreams About Bob

———

Created, collected & edited by

Mary Lee Kortes

BMG BOOKS

<u>Untitled</u>

Meet Dylan we kiss

circa 1965

no, its true, promise

—Gillian McCain

FOREWORD

I dreamed
I had dinner
with
Bob Dylan

in a small
dark restaurant with
brick walls and candles.
The warmth in his eyes was a
guide, a magnet. Without words,
he let me know he liked me and my
music, and, in that silent approval,
encouraged me to keep going. Two
kindred souls, one just happened
to be an icon—an archetype—
and one a not-quite-
complete unknown.

I dreamed I had dinner
with Bob Dylan many times.
One morning it occurred to me that
I couldn't be the only one in this
world dreaming about him. He'd taken up
such wide residence in so many minds.
So I started posting a call, here
and there, for dreams
of Dylan.

Deep sleep is a rich
wilderness, a playground that spawns
battle and discovery, death and rejuvenation,
and, of course, desire—fulfilled and frustrated.
Much has been written about dreams, their interpretation,
symbols, and purpose. No studies on dream symbolism I've found
mention Bob Dylan as a key player. Yet there he is, scampering
through our collective unconscious, sometimes scoundrel, sometimes
savior, and often simply a friend. Collecting and visiting these
115 dreams of Dylan has been a wild pleasure ride. They are
alternately touching, funny, puzzling, wise, crude, tender,
frightening, and romantic. Dreamers treasure them, most of the time.

As he said himself,

"I'll let you be in my dreams
if I can be in yours."

The contributors here have kept their
part of the bargain.

* * *

In the early 1990s, I released a trance-y dance single under
the name Kortez called "Put Your Body On." Visiting my sister in
Michigan for Christmas around that time, I saw a clip on MTV
of Ice Cube talking about his favorite artist of the year.
"Wouldn't it be wonderful to be someone's favorite artist,"
I thought. "If I could be anyone's..."

My mind involuntarily morphed the image on the screen into
Bob Dylan announcing that his favorite of the year was a
new artist called Kortez. This would have been impossible for
any number of reasons—not the least of which was the fact
that the sum total of my released work at the time was that
one single—but that's what fantasies are for. We watched the
snow fall outside my sister's window, changed the channel,
opened our presents, and life went on.

A little over a decade later, a live song-for-song performance
I'd done of <u>Blood on the Tracks</u> was released to much acclaim.
Radio stations around the world played the record. Magazines
heralded my bravery (if they only knew how many times I'd nearly
cancelled that show!). My version of "You're A Big Girl Now"
was featured on Dylan's own web site for months.

And <u>Rolling Stone</u> gave me four stars. That review featured a
large color photo of me with an incredible caption underneath.
In big bold type it proclaimed, "DYLAN FAVE." I had long
since forgotten my television hallucination, but something
else had not. Some dreams do come true.

Mary Lee Kortes

BROOKLYN, NY · SEPTEMBER 2018

I was rehearsing for a Losers Lounge show (an NYC series that takes place at Joe's Pub). I was scheduled to sing Townes Van Zandt's "No Place to Fall" and was rehearsing with the guy who was going to accompany me—Bob Dylan.

We were in a dark, dirty white room, just the two of us. He was sitting on the floor strumming a lute and playing the song in a weird key.

"That's the wrong key," I told him. "I sing it in D. What key are you playing it in?"

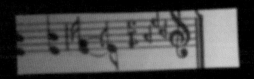

He looked up at me. "The key of I."

I was so annoyed. "There's no such thing," I said.

"That's the key I play it in," said Bob.

Mary Lee Kortes

MUSICIAN, AUTHOR · BROOKLYN, NY

I had a dream
I was walking
amongst people.

They were all
Dylanesque.

I was hoping
to see Bob,
but I just
kept walking.

Michael
Crampton

RETIRED POSTMAN
ADELAIDE,
SOUTH AUSTRALIA

17

BOB, GEORGE, AND LIONEL

David Sallach

SOCIAL SCIENTIST
CHICAGO, IL

George Will reviewed a new young Dylan in glowing terms, and threw some appreciative comments to the old along the way. The new Dylan had the old one's gifts for flashing imagery, but applied them in an unorthodox, conservative way.

I was in a small fishing village and had to drive back to the city. The new Dylan needed a ride, and I was to pick him up at the Will summerhouse. Two older-generation Will men were there, along with a cherubic looking new young Dylan. All the Wills were friendly. I was also picking up three dogs to ride along. Dylan rode back with me to my house to get them.

The three Wills stopped by. George was looking for a cup of coffee. I offered to make a pot of Mr. Coffee, and he accepted. I was looking through the hutch for a spoon, but the spoon was in the dishwasher. So I gave young Dylan a fork from the same set so George could identify the right spoon.

Father Will had a corncob pipe, and the mood was very friendly and supportive. Father and grandfather Will had very warm eyes and were delighted to see the creativity unfolding among the three younger participants. George had a great sense of humor.

Young Dylan was delighted to discover a group like us. With George's support and help, we were heading for some joyful destiny. I woke with the song/words "Everyone you meet is dancing in the street, all night long" by Lionel Ritchie in my head.

103 | DYLAN VS. PAULSEN

I am sitting at the kitchen table
with my parents. I'm very young in the
dream, only 7 or 8 years old, and
the presidential election is coming.
My parents are fighting about who to
vote for: Bob Dylan or Pat Paulsen.
*name withheld

15 | DOG DREAM

In the spring of 1971, upon awakening,
me and Sam Shepard discovered that we had
both dreamed of Bob Dylan. Mine was so
unusual that Sam suggested that I write
about it. I wrote a kind of nursery song
which I have performed through the years.
Each time I am transported to that very
morning, when the winged dog of Bob Dylan
flew into my dreams.

Patti Smith

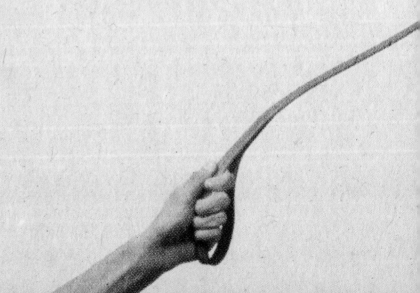

Have you seen Dylan's dog
it got wings it can fly
if you speak of it to him
it's the only time Dylan
can't look you in the eye

Have you held
Dylan's snake
it rattles like a toy
it sleeps in the grass
it coils in his hand
it hums and it strikes out
when Dylan cries out
when Dylan cries out

Have you pressed to your face
Dylan's bird Dylan's bird
it lies on Dylan's hip
it trembles inside of him
it drops upon the ground
it rolls with Dylan round
it's the only one who comes
when Dylan comes

Have you seen Dylan's dog
it got wings it can fly
when it lands like a cloud
it's the only one allowed
to look Dylan in the eye

75 | DON'T PUSH IT

We were somewhere in California, perhaps a coffee shop around
Malibu. In the dream we spoke briefly, and he acknowledged my
presence as not being too bothersome.

Sullio

NEW YORK, NY

36 | POOL BOY

Warren Zanes

WRITER/MUSICIAN · MONTCLAIR, NJ

Here's what you don't want to hear when
conducting interviews for a book project:
"I'm going to tell you a great story...
but you can't use it." When I hear this
I think, "You know I'm gathering material
for a book, right, that I'm not just here
for the hang?" The worst of it
is that these stories are quite often,
and as described, <u>great</u>.
And how often have the "great stories"
been about Bob Dylan? Often.

Tom Petty would share some good Dylan stories. He may not have
flaunted it in public, but Petty was a first-rate storyteller.
He told Dylan stories with relish, affection, and wry humor.
And then he'd say, "But you can't use that."

At the height of writing Petty's biography, I sometimes had
dreams about Petty, some rehashed version of the day's conversations that would have earned Freud's approval. In one dream,
Dylan was featured.

We were backstage in some nondescript arena, road cases lining
the hallways. I was walking with Petty, and he said he was going
to take me to Dylan's dressing room so we could ask permission
to use the stories Petty had been telling me. In the dream I'm
surprised Petty is willing to do this but certainly pleased. We
keep walking and walking and seem to be going ever deeper into
the guts of the venue. I begin feeling that I won't be able to
find my way back, but Petty seems sure of where he is. Finally,
he stops in front of a door with a star on it.

Petty knocks. Someone opens the door. It's Sammy Davis, Jr.
Petty says, "Hey, Sammy, have you seen Bob?" Sammy points further down the hallway and shuts the door, annoyed, like this

has happened too often. Much farther down the hall we arrive at another door. Petty knocks, and his former drummer and sometimes nemesis Stan Lynch opens it. "Hey, have you seen Bob?" Same thing, Lynch points still further down the hallway, shutting the door abruptly. As we're walking away, Petty looks at me and says, "I haven't seen that motherfucker in twenty years."

We continue walking for what again seems a long while. Finally, yet another door with a star. This time, however, Petty tells me to knock. I do. No answer. Then Petty tells me to see if it's open. It is. As I start to pull the door back and peer into a dark room, Petty pushes me in. Next thing I know, I'm in the dark and Petty is laughing out in the hallway. He's shut the door behind me. I feel for the knob, and it's locked. Claustrophobic, about to pound on the door, I start to call out to Petty when I find I can't speak because someone has grabbed me in a chokehold from behind.

I feel a hairy arm around my throat. I hear Dylan's voice, right there in my ear, a hot whisper, his belly in my lower back. "You want stories?" he asks. "Tom says you're looking around for some stories." His hold tightens. "Here's one, pool boy." I wake up.

I walked into this place, not a real nice place, wooden floors all dull and old. A guy was next to me, but I saw a guy on the couch and went to sit next to him. It was Bob Dylan. We started talking, but I couldn't hear him very well. He said something like, "Are you with those people over there?" I said, "No." Then he was saying something else to me, but I couldn't hear him. So I put my hand on his leg and was leaning in real close to him when I noticed that someone had sat down on the other side of me, real close. I turned to look at him—like, "Um, you are interrupting." Then I saw it was Neil Young. That would have been OK.

Trish Rodenbaugh

POST OFFICE · NEW JERSEY

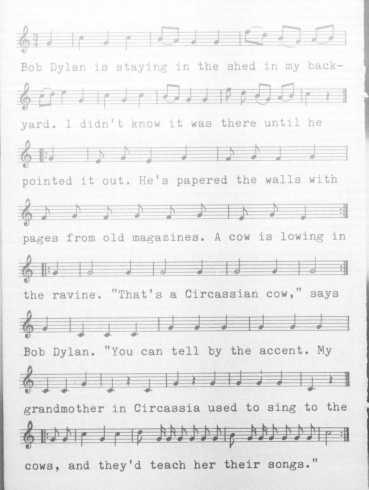

3 | CIRCASSIAN COW

Morten Jonsson

FOOD TECHNOLOGIST · MICHIGAN CITY, IN

I have dreamt of him asking me the meaning of past lives. I explained this to him and how it can make things fall into place. He thanked me and invited me to a new farm he bought.

Eva

AMSTERDAM, THE NETHERLANDS

9 | THE SINGING FOOT

I was walking on a sidewalk in a
business district, looking in the
shop windows. A friend of mine from
my organized religious days was in
a room that could be seen from the
front shop window. She was dressed
up Shabbat and was setting the
table with a lot of sweets. Dylan
walked up behind me, and I took my
shoe off, bent my leg so that the
bottom of my foot was facing him,
and my foot started singing to him,
"It's All Over Now, Baby Blue."

M. C. Israel

UNIVERSITY OF MICHIGAN

12 | A PROM WITH BOB

Rick Danko did kiss my hand (not a
dream), once (four times really),
so that's something.

My dream:
I've never gone to the
prom, or wanted to,
but I had a dream that
I went with Bob Dylan.

It was the late '70s.
I remember just sitting
there with him, maybe
touching hands and
being very happy.

Carol Bertolotti

5

———

DOESN'T PLAY WELL WITH OTHERS

One night I dreamed that
I was working as a lifeguard
in a waterpark at the top of
a very tall slide. Bob was in
line and kept trying to cut
in front of the kids ahead.
I had to keep telling him to
keep his place in line.

M. Willbury

64 | SLITHER

I was at the rail at Bob Dylan's show at the Odyssey, Belfast, Northern Ireland, on June 26, 2004. I'm a big guy, 180 pounds with a large round head, and made a bit of a spectacle of myself singing along on "Moonlight" and other songs. Then during the intermission I yelled out a large, searching

"mmm-ooooooooooo-oh oh oh oh oh oh oh oh oh o-er!"

I later dreamed about that concert and that Dylan said something like, "The stuff I have to put up with," as he passed Stu Kimball. Stu leaned forward, as if saying "What?" causing Bob to run his left hand up Stu's buttons, still walking to center stage in front of George Receli, where I dream he said, "There's the snake," looking at me. George said "What?" at which Bob bent over in a belly laugh at the de-referencing effect of the moonlight. He then turned around to talk to George, saying something like, "No, you guys are OK. This would work far better without the crowd." Then he returned to his keyboard and went a few steps backstage, removed his hat, and patted the top of his head saying, "Need to check the snake hasn't got in here."

S. McC.

ADMINISTRATIVE ASSISTANT · ANTRIM, IRELAND

96

COME HERE,
LEAVE ME ALONE

He was singing a ballad, intimately, and I walked
over to the benches. I was with someone, and we were
able to stand right in front of Dylan. I became
tearful because the song was so beautiful. Then,
when it ended, Dylan handed me a camera and asked me
to take his photo. It had a long lens, like a tele-
scope, and I couldn't work out how to use it. I was
confused and started to take multiple photos of him,
although he looked miles away through the lens.
He became annoyed because I took too many photos.

Craig Beaumont

CONSULTANT · NEW YORK, NY

I dreamed once that I am in hospital and I had to stay for some days. On one day, there was Dylan, clothed as a nurse.

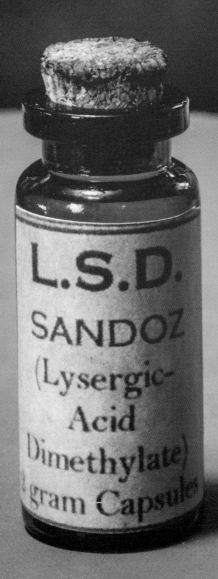
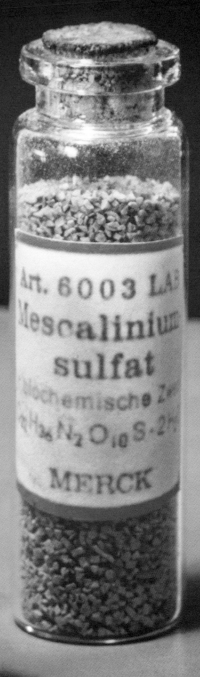

Patrick Aeschbach

THE NETHERLANDS

61 | VISIONARY

I have had many dreams about Dylan,
and he has never spoken to me in them
until recently when he named a hill near
where I grew up. "You can see the sea
from there," he said. But you can't.

Geoff Ward

WRITER, SINGER/SONGWRITER · IRELAND

10 | THE WALL

A bunch of us were stuck on the southern side of
the Wall and the US government was paying Mexico
to keep us in jail. Bob kept coming to me because
he kept losing harmonicas, and I'm a scrounger.
Some of us managed to escape but couldn't get over
the wall. Bob was always losing his harmonica.
I knew of a tunnel in Nuevo Laredo that ran under
a Laundromat to the US side and managed to smug-
gle Bob back into America, despite all of Trump's
efforts to keep him out. I became a national hero,
received cash and acclaim. Bob held a benefit
concert/press interview where he stated I was the
best harmonica player he had ever heard and wanted
me to play at all his upcoming concerts. I immediately returned to Mexico.

Lee Winkle

PLUMBER · IRVING, TX

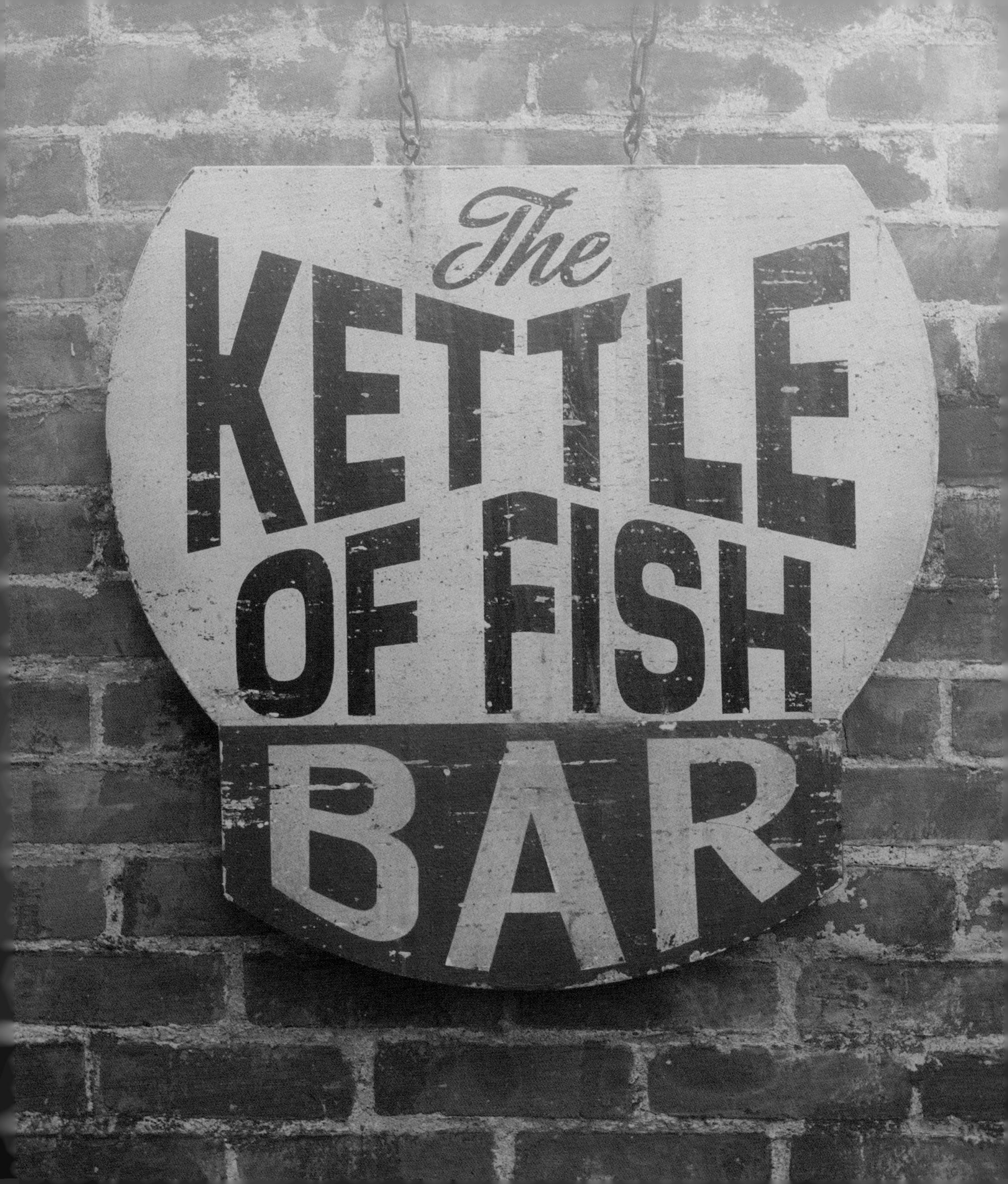
The
KETTLE
OF FISH
BAR

27

PROPER PLACE SETTING

I'm leaning on a bar talking to a friend of mine about a tuning fork that he had just given me as a gift for my birthday. I tapped the tuning fork on the side of my hand and placed it quickly up to my ear. Doing this, my head turned slightly sideways, and my eye caught Bob standing at the far end of the bar talking to Tony Garnier and Harlan Howard, who was writing something on a bar napkin. It seemed that I was then caught in Bob's sightlines, and he reached over and stopped Harlan for a second, looked over at us again, and said, "Hey guys, you got a knife with that fork?"

Ian Charles

Chris MacCormick

ADMISSIONS DIRECTOR,
RESIDENTIAL
TREATMENT CENTER
AURORA, NY

6 | BOB TEACHES BOATING

I was on an island, bound to stay awhile. I went to visit
a young Bob Dylan. It was less trouble than expected to get
in to see him, because his thing for the day was teaching a
class about boats to anyone who signed up. We waited for him
in an untidy studio, in the center of which rows of desks had
been set up, and looked at the paintings that were standing
around. Most were recognizably by him and not very compelling,
but there was a large one, neatly hung, that was more subdued
and elegant. Its subject was unclear, but it might have been
of children playing a game on a foggy hillside. I liked it

a lot but wasn't sure he could have painted
it until I had studied it closely in the dim
light and discovered traces of his writing
under the surface, which was burnished to
the point that it almost seemed to glow.

When he entered, the desks filled up with
young fans. Right away he passed out a
quiz we were to complete at the end of his
lecture. He was much more serious about boats
and sailing than anyone had anticipated. I
found some of his concepts difficult. There
was a lot of math, and his presentation was
so vivid and imaginative. I really wanted
just to listen and not worry about retaining
any of the information, but it was clear that
would not be acceptable. The quiz turned out
to be not so much of a problem for me, since
a friend was sitting at the next desk and
I could look at her work and cheat. Several
others complained aloud, though. I sympathized
with them, while feeling rather ungrateful
to him on that account. He responded to their
challenges with a wonderful, harshly funny
rap that made me—and by their looks, everyone
else—feel privileged to have been a witness.

16 | GEAR SHOPPING

I was shopping in a musical instrument store (which I do
frequently) with Bob Dylan (which I have never done).
I think we were mostly looking at guitars. There was a
very pushy and obnoxious salesman who was "helping" us,
but he eventually got so annoying that Bob said
(in the nasal voice everyone uses when imitating him)
"I think I better LEEEAVE before you try to sell MEEE!"

Dave Meinzer

GRAPHIC DESIGNER · BUFFALO, NY

91 | DON'T WORRY, BABY

It was morning. I was in a room somewhere with Dylan.
It was supposed to be his studio, I think. There was a bed
or sofa or daybed. We were laying on it. I was asleep, and
he was stroking my head. I kept wondering if I was dreaming
or imagining it. Then he would do it again, as if to say,
"Don't worry. What does it matter? I'm here now."
A wonderful feeling. Then we got up, and I was walking
around kind of sleepy and dazed. There were other people
there. I was wondering if they were wondering if we'd slept
together. But this was better than sex. This was love,
true intimacy, tenderness. I was high for days.

Name withheld

NEW YORK, NY

81 | O CAPTAIN

I was invited together with a lot of
others to enter a slow train that was
arriving. We all boarded, and it started
to move forward. Suddenly, it wasn't a
train anymore; it was transformed into
a plane, and I was the only passenger.
The top, sides, and floor fell off.
Then I saw the captain of the plane
was Dylan. He smiled wickedly, and off
he went, leaving me alone up there in
space, in the dark, paralyzed.

Tuulikki Bogman

SOCIAL WORKER
STOCKHOLM, SWEDEN

113 | NOT ALONE

I was walking around a city
at dark with Bob Dylan and
Jim Morrison. It was lined
with amber-colored street-
lights and kind of foggy.
I don't remember what was
said, but I do recall
thinking Dylan didn't like
me much.

Jeremy Wobbe

79 FISHING

I once dreamed I was riding my motorcycle along some winding country road, speeding into the curves like a wild man, and suddenly I came around this hairpin curve, and there was this little guy in a leather jacket in front of me on some kind of Harley. I had this little rubber ball on a long elastic string, so I took it out of my dresser, which I was pulling behind me with a rope, and started flinging it at the other guy's helmet. As I was laughing my ass off, I noticed flashing lights behind me. I quickly pulled to the middle of the road and stopped. I hadn't noticed the siren before, but as I turned around, I realized it was blaring "Copper Kettle," and the police officer was Dylan, coming right up to me with a billy club and a can of smoked salmon. He asked to see my fishing license, and I told him that I forgot to bring it along. Then he told me to stand up, turn around, and put my hands behind my back. I felt something snap into my hands, and it was a fishing pole. Then he started drilling me on fishing techniques, having me cast into the woods and bring back an oak leaf, a maple leaf, a rabbit—all kinds of things—and I didn't even have a treble hook, so it was pretty hard to do. Finally, he issued me a temporary fishing permit, just in case I got stopped again on the way home, and I headed back to my bike, but the engine had fallen off and melted down through the asphalt, and Dylan was yelling at some old lady for taking too long to cross the street.

*name withheld

77 | PICKUP?

My dream was that my wife and I were staying for a couple days at this cabin in the woods. Well, who should be there but Dylan, circa 1966. I spent most of the dream trying to keep my wife (not terribly fond of him, but with some grudging respect) and Dylan apart for fear that he'd say something truly devastating to her. I suddenly realized I was alone in the room, and out the front window I saw Dylan and my wife standing in back of his red pickup talking very amicably. My relief and curiosity were so intense I woke up.

Timothy Lundgren

OHIO STATE UNIVERSITY

In a dream, I visit a Civil War battle-field. I tour it alone, walking over the ground wondering who might be buried below my feet. It is daytime.

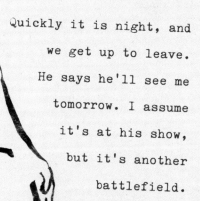

Bob appears, also walking alone. As he gets closer, he acknowledges me, saying he recognizes me from some shows. I tell him I saw him make a point to remember my face.

Quickly it is night, and we get up to leave. He says he'll see me tomorrow. I assume it's at his show, but it's another battlefield.

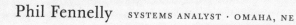

Phil Fennelly SYSTEMS ANALYST · OMAHA, NE

1 | DYLAN WAS A WOMAN

But even in my dream I was confused
Because I knew Dylan is a man
And not a woman
But I knew this was a dream
And in a dream he can be a woman
And then I played some Dylan music
A live show from twenty years ago
And she said
That it gives her a headache
That her old songs
Give her a headache.
Then Dylan hugged me
And I asked whispering in her ear
If she is Van Morrison's girlfriend
She laughed
Or maybe it was he
Or both
He or she laughed
And said yes they're friends
But they fight all the time
She kept hugging me
And then I said
Like two kids
Who fight all the time
Next thing Dylan
Wanted me to come to New York
She invites me
She is sending tickets
She's in love with me.
My wife was mad

In the beginning there was Van
    Morrison's music
And Dylan spoke to my wife
Dylan had a decent ass in spite of
    looking fifty years old
I thought she (Dylan) had plastic
    surgery
Money was never a problem for her
For this Dylan

Mois Benarroch

POET · ISRAEL

97 | TOUCH

I was at a concert, and a fight broke out when Dylan appeared
on stage and performed a very slow, quiet drum solo. The men
across from me began to abuse him, somebody heckled them, and
suddenly there was an enormous fight. The stage emptied, and
when Dylan returned, he proceeded to talk to the audience.
There were many empty rows, and I moved closer, three or four
rows from the front. Suddenly I was next to him, talking to
him. He was laughing at something, and he touched me on the
forehead and then walked away. I was gobsmacked.

Craig Beaumont

CONSULTANT · NEW YORK, NY

42 | KISS

I dreamed I met Bob in 2004. I had front row seats. I didn't
know I was going to be on the side with him and his keyboard.
He stood in front of me all night long until the concert
ended. And then he did the line up with his band members.
I shouted out loud to Tony Garnier who was by him in the line
up. I pointed to Tony and said, "Tell Bob to come over here."

Tony pointed to me and told Bob to go over to me. Bob walked
slowly over, near his keyboard. He kneeled down first and
shook my hand and said, "Hi. What's ya name?" "Jeana," I said.

So we talked a little bit more, and after our conversation,
he was about to leave. And then he got closer to my face,
and he gave me a kiss right on the lips. I almost passed out
that he did that. But I'm glad it happened.

Jeana

CHARLESTON, SC

Jeff Ogiba

CO-OWNER, BLACK GOLD RECORDS
BROOKLYN, NY

I find myself standing in a former apartment in the
suburbs of New Jersey. The silhouette of a man with wild and
curly hair sits in a grey cloud of smoke with his back facing me.
As I approach him, I realize he is very faintly playing an acoustic
guitar. I can't make out the notes, and in listening I notice that
he is softly humming lyrics. He turns to me, and the smoke clears.
I'm shocked to see that I am standing face to face with a mid-1970s
Bob Dylan. He's turned to eye makeup, he's beginning to wrinkle,
and he's wearing some really stupid hat. "You wanna hear a new one,
Jeff?" he asks me as he exhales, adding to the plume that has now
filled the room. "Sure!" I said as I sat down on this tiny couch
about ten feet from where he was sitting.

They call me a poet / But I too love me some prose
I'll bet half a dollar / Donald Trump got dirty toes

I was partially thrilled to hear this new work, yet confused by
the timely topic he chose to sing about. It then became very clear
(and extremely confusing) to me that Mr. Dylan and I had been very
close friends since well before I was born. I offered him a beer
from my fridge, but all I found when I opened the refrigerator door
were two empty plastic six pack rings and a rotisserie chicken.
The chicken rolled over and looked up me. It's neck hole spoke
in whispers, "Thisss is a dreeeeeam, Jeffy. Dylan don't eeeeven
knoooow you exissssst!" I woke up on my couch, Tarantula on the
floor and a post-game report on the television with Keith Hernandez
complaining about how badly the Mets lost. I was upset to have
woken up to so many disappointments, but glad Bob didn't
actually write anything like my dream suggested.

And I was playing matchmaker. Amusing for a very reform Jewish girl to have a dream that she is inviting Bob Dylan to her childhood home for Shabbat dinner—a home where there never was a Friday night Shabbat dinner, ever—but here was my subconscious having one with Bob Dylan as a guest. We were in our white house in Ohio—with my mom and dad (not currently married) who were perfectly fine to be at this Shabbat dinner in the place where we'd lived as a nuclear family for years without one.

And there I was, matchmaker in reverse: me on a mission, looking for a "mensch" for my mom. Before dinner started, my mom and Bob were flirting a little bit, really hitting it off! I thought, "That's convenient and great! Bob is an artsy guy, and my mom likes artsy guys, and I'm sure he's got some sort of financial stability, which will be

good for her also." I con-
gratulated my matchmaking self. After all, I was
trying to get Bob to come to the Shabbat dinner
to meet my mom, and he did!

My dad was not too pleased with this situation
though, and not because he was watching my mom
and Bob flirt. As a huge music fan, he wanted
Bob's attention, but Bob was giving it all to
my mom. My dad couldn't believe he was in his
own house—at Shabbat dinner no less—and here
was Bob Dylan, one of his musical heroes, acting
like he wasn't even there.

Meanwhile I was trying to gauge the probability
that my mom and Bob might become an item. I was
really rooting for it because I thought it would
be great for her. I don't remember how the dream
ended, but I did write a song about it:

I had a dream that Bob Dylan
    had a crush on my mom.
And my dad was envious 'cause Bob
    couldn't recognize his charm.
And I said, "Mom is single,
    and she is cute to boot!"

Alyson Greenfield

SINGER/SONGWRITER,
PROFESSOR · BROOKLYN, NY

MY MOM

ONE GOOD TURN

Bob and I are sitting on a park bench
and chatting, about music, the weather,
etc. It was well on its way to becoming
just another unremarkable Bob sighting.
But then I noticed that my car had a
flat tire. "Great," I said, "I don't
have a jack." Bob replied, "Hey, don't
worry, I got one," and walked over to
his own car. He brought over the jack
and helped me change the tire.

"Hey, thanks, Bob," I said.

"Nah,
don't worry
about it,
you'll do
the same for me
sometime."

Mike Fornatele

MUSICIAN · RIVER VALE, NJ

112 | ANAGRAM

I dreamed Bob and I were having a
great conversation backstage somewhere—
well, I did all the talking, and
he just smiled a lot, which was
enough for me!
Then I pointed out to him
that my first name is an anagram
of his last.

Lynda Glen

YOGA TEACHER & MASSAGE THERAPIST
SYDNEY, AUSTRALIA

Bob was playing in the local country hall, a very small building surrounded by green fields and grazing sheep and cattle on the main road about two miles from my parents' farm. The hall was filled with the local country people, the kids I had been to school with and their parents. Rex Fenemore was there, Colin Taplin was there, and the Bubbs, a big local family. The band was setting up on the tiny stage, and there were colored streamers hanging down from the ceiling. It was Bob's Budokan band, and they were having trouble getting everyone into such a small space. We waited and waited, and as the time for Bob to come on drew near, a strange thing happened.

All the local people started drifting away. One by one they all left. The band members seemed to disappear as well. Finally, there was only me and Bob in the whole hall. He went on stage, picked up his guitar, and looked out over the tiny empty hall. Empty, except for me. I waited for Bob to start singing. He looked at me awhile, and then he said: "Bugger this, it's not worth it. I'll drive you home."

14 | WALKING THE ROOM

We went outside and got into my parents' big dirty red Holden Belmont—a real farmer's car. Bob revved it up with me next to him in the front seat of the car, and sped towards the bridge on the little road that leads to the house.

There have been other dreams. Great concerts in strange and shifting venues: the one on the lonely beach; the one illuminated by fire; the one in the tiny living room where Bob had to be coaxed to sing; the one in the great big supertop tent—oh right, that was real.

Andrew McCallum

SENIOR ANALYST, MINISTRY OF ECONOMIC
DEVELOPMENT · NEW ZEALAND

Scott Kempner

SONGWRITER/GUITARIST/SINGER

SANTA BARBARA, CA

When I heard the triple knock at my door, followed by the double
knock in perfect cadence, I knew it was Bob. The triple/double knock
that is shorthand for "Louie Louie" was known only to our immediate
friends, our fans, management and road crew—the insider's code to
signal it was friend not foe at the door—and he or she was cleared
for entry. Yes, even in my dream I knew all that. And, since everyone
else was already inside, it could only be Bob, a bit late, but still,
a fully cleared friend and musical brother. I wondered what he wanted
this time. Given that it was nearing 4 AM I figured it was a baseball
trivia question, for which $10 always hung in the balance.

 Bob had really gone for Baseball Weekly, the stat- and opinion-
heavy newspaper dedicated to nothing but baseball. He'd love to come
across some arcane statistic and try to lighten my load by ten bucks.
But I was pretty good at this game myself, having grown up in the

shadow of Yankee Stadium during the Mantle/Maris years, and having

been to at least 100-125 games by the end of the 1963 season. This

was how my third Bob Dylan dream of the week began.

Whenever Bob would show up, if you listened carefully, you could

hear any number of Bob compositions playing in your head. That day it

was "Chimes of Freedom." As usual, first thing Bob asked was how did

the Yankees do that day. I told him we'd won. I checked the game's

box score, as Bob looked over my shoulder and gave a little "whoop"

when he noticed a particularly favorable stat that pleased him.

Mantle had hit a 445-foot home run that day.

Suddenly, it was three days later (same dream, though). Then came

a 3 AM knock on the door. It was the "Louie Louie" knock. I yelled,

"Bob, it's 3 AM!!" I heard the sound of scurrying feet, and by the

time I got to the door, the hallway was silent and empty.

I looked down to see a mailing tube with the address crossed out

and the notation, "Here it is, I am offering 10-1 odds if someone can

solve this mystery!!" Hmmmmm??!!

Inside the tube was a rolled-up copy of a month-old Baseball Weekly.

So, any remaining mystery as to who had left this on my doorstep was

solved. I picked up the magazine, and a small envelope fell out.

Inside was a cryptic message—"121714"—and out came a single $100

bill! "What the...?"

I took it back inside with me and went back to bed. It was now

3:15 AM, but I couldn't get back to sleep. These six digits, the

promise of 10-1 odds to solve their meaning, and the one hundred

smackers that could soon be mine kept me awake. So, was I looking

at a potential of turning that $100 into $1,000? I never knew Bob

to mislead me with his quizzes and punchlines, so I rid my brain of

those particular thoughts.

Even at this hour, I was completely cognizant that Bob was a

diehard Yankees fan, like me. So that was where I would start and—

hopefully—end my investigation. 121714? I was too tired to go to

my computer to see if I could cut to the chase, so I just laid

there wide awake and thought about it, over and over.

I went to the bookshelf, pulled out the Baseball Encyclopedia, and

looked up Mickey's stats. As I scoured the obvious and the intri-

cate stats, something caught my eye: in Mickey's final three sea-

sons—1966, '67, and '68—he had hit, in order, 12 doubles, 17 doubles

and 14 doubles. There it was! Bob had challenged me to figure out

that Mantle's last three seasons' doubles totals were the answer to the mystery. And, by the time I woke up at 9 AM, once again to the "Louie Louie" knock, there was an envelope sitting wedged between my door and the door frame. Inside was indeed a rubber band-wrapped pile of ten $100 bills, crisp and new. Now, that was a good way to start the morning after a most surreal night. Bob knew I would solve this one.

It wasn't until a week later that I ran into Bob. He was returning from breakfast with fellow Greenwich Village folk singer and story-teller Dave Van Ronk. Dylan confessed he'd been given that exact challenge by Van Ronk—who did not put up a $1,000 prize, but had put up a $10,000 prize, as that was half the amount he said he'd made from the Animals' version of "House of the Rising Sun." Dave picked up the tab. So Bob had some fun, a free breakfast, and a new Yankees stat he could use to amaze his friends. Bob did pay the tip on that breakfast, though. Or so he said.

* * *

P.S.—Despite this being a dream, I _did_ grow up in the shadow of Yankee stadium and _did_ attend over 100 games by 1953. This was my _third_ Dylan dream of that week, and I have _no idea_ if Dave Van Ronk ever made anything from that Animals' recording!

John Howells

OWNER, PUNK HART PRODUCTIONS

COTTAGE GROVE, OR

21 | PRESIDENT BOB

Dylan had been elected President in 1976 and came into office with grand plans and schemes for making the country great again after Nixon and Watergate.

Soon he lost interest, and after having failed to get any of his programs through Congress, he pretty much fizzled out and declined to run for another term.

His entire term in office was considered a failure best forgotten.

4 | BLOOD BROTHERS

I dreamed I was in a room with Bob Dylan. He had a pocketknife and was doing that thing where you spread your fingers on a table and rapidly stab the knife between your fingers, back and forth, over and over. He stabbed a finger on his left hand, and it bled all over the table. He shook his hand and blood splattered on my hand. He never said a word.

Gene Goodale   PRE-PRESS OPERATOR · BROCKTON, MA

26 | DEATH IS NOT AN OWIE

I'm on the phone with my brother talking about our sick mother, who's in the hospital near death (that part's true). I don't think he's really facing the fact that she's dying and the difficulty that's bringing up for him (also true), and I tell him, "Death is not an owie." I decide that this is an outstanding book title and that I should write that book. I start planning the sections and how I'll talk about grief. But when I remember I'm not a grief specialist, I realize I'd better write it more as a memoir so I can write with authority and authenticity. I present my idea to a publisher, who becomes interested. We're in a restaurant at a big table with people from the editorial board of the publishing company, which includes Bob Dylan. He turns to me and says, "Your book needs more work."

Sarah Spacsh

CHILD PSYCHOTHERAPIST/WRITER

DES MOINES, IA

23 | ANGEL BOB

Dylan is sitting in the audience at a concert wearing angel wings, and Jakob Dylan is on stage performing, "If You See Her, Say Hello."

Kathryn

SOCIAL SERVICES · NEW YORK

108 | SURPRISE!

Ken West

I dreamed I was onstage with Dylan playing drums, but just as the song began, I realized that I don't know how to play drums.

50 | L'AMOUR

I saw him alone in a studio, playing guitar and singing to the melody
of "Standing in the Doorway" a sentence that's probably from Jacques
Lacan: "Aimer c'est donner ce qu'on n'a pas," which means something
like "love means to give what you don't possess." *name withheld

109 | IT'S TIME

I was on a big boat, like a luxury liner,
asleep in a big open room on a lower level on
a mattress on the floor. Dylan called me on my
cell phone to tell me it was time to get up.
Then my real-life cell phone alarm went off,
interrupting my dream of Dylan calling me on my
cell phone to tell me it was time to get up.

He knows everything.

Mary Lee Kortes

MUSICIAN, AUTHOR · BROOKLYN, NY

I was somewhere, with all my friends I
believe, and Bob Dylan was performing,
but it was just in this building, and he
had his own desk along with some other
people. After he performed, he hung up
his guitar on the wall. When he was all
alone after he performed, I went up to
him and introduced myself and told him
I was a big fan. We talked for a while,
but then I had to go, and he gave me his
number so that we could talk again.

I called him and told him about my life.
I told him about two business plans I
had, and he was really interested. But as
I was telling him about another, we got
disconnected, and people were waiting for
me at the dinner table, so I had to go.

Andrew

BUSINESS STUDENT · MINNEAPOLIS, MN

41 | WAITING

I was in a sort of bar/restaurant/general store. It
might have been New Orleans. It had a country and
western theme. I saw Bob milling around, checking
the place out. He was anonymous to the rest of the
people in the establishment. I approached him ner-
vously, expecting to be turned away. He was fairly
amiable as we struck up a conversation about the
honky-tonk band that was playing. At one point he
seemed slightly exasperated with me, but only for a
moment. I suggested that we take the stage and join
the band for a song. He agreed immediately. We separated to get our instruments. I went upstairs and
then returned although I was carrying no instrument, but there was no sign of Bob. I waited for
what seemed like only a few seconds, but he never
showed up. I felt mildly disillusioned, and so I
left the building.

Henry Porter

19 | MR. JONES

I work as a writer for a
magazine. I have interviewed
quite a few musicians,
but never Dylan.

I dream that my editor
and a friend of his had
arranged a meeting with
Dylan at a restaurant.
They asked me to come
along because (in the
dream) I had interviewed
him once before. They
thought I would help
break the ice. I was
the last to arrive at a
table in a nondescript
New York coffee shop. I
took a seat across from
Dylan. He looked just
like he does now, weary,
lines on his face. I
tried to say something
funny, but whatever it
was, it came out lame.
Dylan looked at me with
a blank expression. I
realized he was mocking
me. An awkward silence
fell over the table. I
realized I was Mr. Jones.

*name withheld

110 | IT'LL COST YOU

I had a dream that 1965 Bob Dylan and I were in a relationship, and he asked me to be pregnant. I asked for one million dollars first, and he complied. When I woke up, I immediately started laughing. I also had another dream that 1990s Bob came to my campus and was talking with a group of my friends who had no idea who he was. So I introduced myself, and we talked on our way to the football field bleachers. He laughed about everything I said, but he would only talk about sea lions, which confused me immensely, even in my dream.

Skyla Marie Puckett

PSYCHOLOGY MAJOR
UNIVERSITY OF WEST GEORGIA

115 | SHOOT

I am walking down the main drag in Boise, Idaho (never been). I hear loud, rapid clicking and scuffling behind me. I turn around, and Bob Dylan is aggressively photographing me, running back and forth on the sidewalk, kneeling, leaning from side to side on his toes. It looks like he has an expensive professional camera, but he comes up to me and pulls some polaroid shots out of his pocket and says, "Five dollars." Although he was photographing me from the back, the pictures are all of my face, and I am crying.

Reinga Davenpoort

PASTOR · STATEN ISLAND, NY

90 | TOO CLOSE

I knocked on this door and Bob answered it and
let me in. He was talking to someone, but in my
mind, we were getting close, getting to know each
other. That's the only way I can explain what
I did next because I would never have done this
if I'd just met Bob Dylan: he was standing there
in front of me and I wrapped my arms around his
waist and was squeezing him, but then I woke up.
I think I made us both uncomfortable.

Trish Rodenbaugh

POST OFFICE · NEW JERSEY

87 | VISITATION

I was a close friend of Bruce Langhorne.
After he died, I had this dream:

I've just had a baby.
Bob Dylan comes to visit and wants to be my lover.
I have so many people in my space.
They won't leave me alone.
I have video of the birth that I want to show Dylan,
  but I can't get the people to leave.
I put signs up. I go and yell at them about their
  intrusiveness.
When I go back to my space, Dylan has left.

Dylan comes back to visit and support Bruce
  at the end of his life.

Cynthia Riddle

FILMMAKER · REDONDO BEACH, CA

63 | CLEAN

Bob and I are
in this huge but very
intimate bathtub. Yes, we are
naked. The candlelit bathroom is
made of mostly dark wood, and right next
to the tub are three giant windows revealing
darkness and trees blowing in the wind (I know).
Here is the amazing part: I'm lying on top of him and
he is washing my hair. Washing my hair!!! I remember so
many intimate features of his face from that dream. I don't
know if they are really part of Bob's face. All I know is that I
felt completely relaxed and safe and secure.   *name withheld

8 | MÉNAGE À DREAM

Once my wife dreamed she had sex with Bob. When she
told me that, I was upset and jealous. I would have
loved to have this dream too!!

Nicolas Prum-Duhanot

DENTIST · CLERMONT-FERRAND, FRANCE

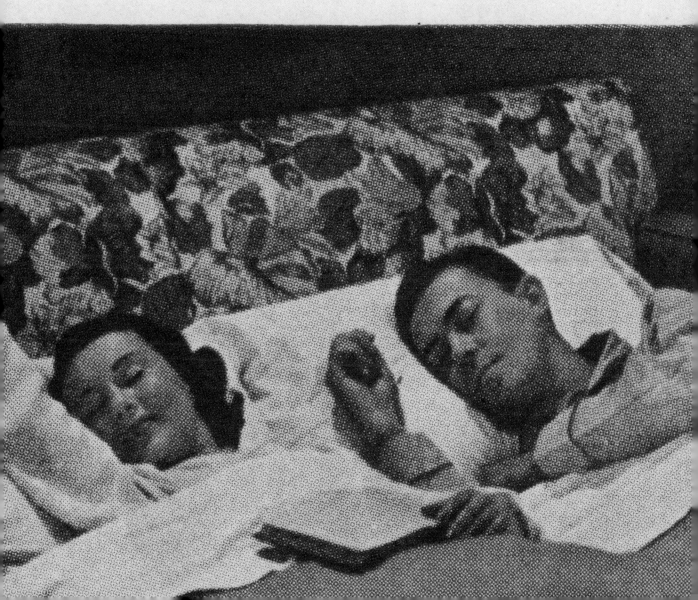

Matthew Taylor
Berntheizel

QUALITY INSPECTOR
COLUMBIA, PA

I passed out dehydrated after a
14-hour tour of duty cutting a problem tree
down—and then up—for a friend, with plenty
of adult libations throughout.

A moment before I awoke from my
deep REMs, I had a flashing dream
of trying to dip a cool drink of
spring water from a seep,

89 | THIRST

but try as I may, the ladle kept coming up dry,
despite the abundance of water before me.

Bob Dylan appeared behind me and said,
"The vandals took the handle."

I angrily turned and said, "It's a spring, and I've got a
ladle. What the hell do I need a pump handle for?"

And he said, "That's a good question."

Dylan was sitting
in the back of a car
in a fur coat.

He asked me through the window,
"Which way's the gig, man?"

I said, "I wouldn't start from here."

He said, "Too clever by half,"
and wound the window up.

45 | FUR

An ex-girlfriend of mine was in the
car with him acting like she didn't know me.
It started to rain, and he drove off.

I got on my bike and followed after,
and somehow I didn't get wet.

John Booth

80 | SOLO

I dreamed Dylan was singing in the middle of a row
of seats. He was in great form, but nobody was there.

Salvatore Licciardello

ITALY

111 | CO-WRITE

I dreamed Bob and I were sitting in a studio writing
a song together. I liked the melody, but I thought
the lyrics could be better, so I told him. He left the
room in a huff, and I went home and changed them.

Kate Hyman

NEW YORK, NY

56 | THANKSGIVING

I dreamed that one day Dylan realized what he's meant
to so many people, and that all over this universe they
just want to say thanks. He can stop running now.

Michael Capanna

MONTREAL

70 | ROASTED GOOSE FEET

Jimbo Mathus

BANDLEADER, SQUIRREL NUT ZIPPERS,
PRODUCER, WRITER · TAYLOR, MS

I was up in Brooklyn visiting my dear friends Mary Lee Kortes and Eric Ambel. Over dinner the first night we were conversing and catching up with one another. Mary Lee told me of her book she was working on of collected dreams contributed by individuals that had Bob Dylan as an essential element. She then began explaining all of the serendipitous ways in which Bob Dylan had actually informed and influenced her life and work. She related several stories that were quite remarkable, causing me to comment, "It sounds like you've got the bob gris-gris on ya." Thinking no more of it, we retired for the night. And then I dreamed of Dylan, for the first time ever.

* * *

I was in an old northern hunting lodge, the type I used to see advertised in my father's stack of <u>Field</u> <u>and</u> <u>Stream</u> magazines that he had saved from the 1950s. They would offer guided hunting

and fishing trips for game that was foreign to my southern ter-

ritory, such as geese, bear, mule, deer, muskellunge, and pike,

and would be in states that also were foreign and mysterious to

me—like Michigan, Wisconsin, and Minnesota. The photos in the

ads showed hunters in the garb of the time: red and black plaid

mackinaws and knee-high lace up hunting boots. In the dream, I

was seated with other guests in the dining hall of the lodge,

which was a wood-paneled, low-ceilinged room. It was dimly lit by

lanterns and had a very medieval, tavern-like feel. The lodge was

about to close down permanently after many years of operation,

and the guests were discussing this as I eavesdropped.

I heard many pondering the fate of the caretaker there and what

would become of him after the shut down. They spoke of him as an

ornery, antisocial, crotchety old dude, but in a fond way.

As this was occurring, a shadowy, hunched-over individual was

passing back and forth through the room with sidelong glances

that alluded to the fact that this individual, the caretaker, was

a certain Bob Dylan. He eventually sat down at a table alone,

separated from other guests. I walked over and engaged him in some conversation. He was preparing to move from the lodge to

an uncertain future and didn't know what he was going to do with

all his "earthly possessions." He commented that he had saved up

many things and wondered if I wanted to take some of them with

me. "Yes," I said, and he proceeded to lead me through the narrow

hallways to the room where he had stored everything. As he pulled

out a ring of keys and opened a small door, we entered a huge,

brightly lit warehouse space that was lined floor to ceiling with

metal shelves. On these shelves sat everything he had amassed. The

shelves actually receded into the far distance, but from what I

could see, they were filled with myriad arcane objects from the

"old, weird America": metal toys and cowboy stuff, old Hollywood

memorabilia, space-age-inspired lamps and decoration, phonographs,

and outdated appliances. I said I couldn't really decide what to

take, and since he was leaving that night, he gave me the key.

We then proceeded through some more corridors, and he said,

"I'll show you the kitchen." We entered another cramped room where

game animals were roasting on metal grates over immense piles of

coals. He said, "These coals have been burning for

99 years."

As this was closing night and the last supper at the lodge, they were clearing the freezers of all the game and roasting them all at once. The strange thing was that on those grates, whole deer of various sizes were being cooked. They hadn't been dressed or butchered, just whole deer lying there. They were actually peacefully sleeping on the forge-like heat of the coals, and you could see them breathing and shifting position slightly as they slept. On smaller grills to the side he showed me the delicacy of the lodge: roasted goose. It was the head and neck of the goose with the feathers still on and "roasted goose feet."

As we went to get his suitcase in his small bedroom, he related that he had been the object of pranks and ridicule from local kids all through the years who found him scary and odd. I noticed as we were walking out that kids had snuck into his room and drawn a cryptic picture on his mattress to curse him as he left.

The drawing resembled Haitian veve symbols. He remarked that he would now have to get this jinx removed before he could travel on to the next place. I said, "Don't worry, Bob. I'll take care of those kids for ya." With that he left, suitcase in hand.

Gris-gris indeed.

8 ♠

34 | CARDS

Geoff Ward

SONGWRITER · IRELAND

10 ♣

My son, then aged 11, and
I meet Dylan in a cabin
or bunkhouse, which has a
stove and beds in it. Dylan
gives us each a playing
card—me, the 8 and my son,
the 10—and each card shows
both spades and clubs. After
Dylan gives us the cards,
he leaves through a door
at the far end, silhou-
etted against an intensely
bright light, possibly sun-
light, without a word.

25 | SWIMMINGLY

I am in a large body of water, sort of treading and holding on up against a large rock. I can see a sandy beach off to the left and want to swim there, but there are large, black pointed metal-looking objects jutting up just under the surface of the water. Then I realize they are hippopotamus sculptures. Then I realize they are actual hippopotamuses, and one of them swims to me and wants me to pet its head. I oblige, and it licks my hand like a cat. All of a sudden, Dylan swims by, stealthily, athletically, skimming across the top of the water, oblivious to the danger lurking below.

Thomas Rowley   CATERER · SARASOTA, FL

13 | HANK № 1

Bob Dylan is in the back seat of my car.
We're going to get some cigarettes and ice
cream. He's telling me about Hank Williams,
how Hank died in the back seat of a car
singing "I Saw the Light." Bob Dylan starts
singing "I Saw the Light," but the tune is
different, somewhere between "La Cucaracha"
and "My Darling Clementine." The words are
different too. I'm not sure they're in English.
I need to ask him what flavor of ice cream
he wants, but I'm afraid to interrupt.

Morten Jonsson

FOOD TECHNOLOGIST · MICHIGAN CITY, IN

I was standing on a corner in Santa Fe singing my own reiterations of Bob Dylan songs for the tourists, which I have been doing all over America for the past 25 years. A big black Bentley limousine pulls up, the window was rolled down, and someone inside was apparently listening to my performance.

Out of the back door of the Bentley jumps Bob Dylan himself! He says: "No, no, that is not how it goes. Let me show you how the chords change." So, speechless and humbled, I give him my guitar, and he proceeded to sing it beautifully but so energetically he breaks the A string.

I suggested right away that he could replace the string, and he replies, "I can do better than that! I like what you are doing, so how about this? This might make you real happy."

He walks back to the Bentley, pulls out an old Martin Dreadnought, and gives it to me, saying "Sorry about your A string." I thank him profusely at this great act of kindness, and then he says to get in the limousine so we can take a cruise in the nicer neighborhoods of Santa Fe.

We headed south to Barcelona Road and pulled into the synagogue, with Bob saying, "You know I am still Jewish, although I totally have my own religion."

"Tell me about it, please," I prompted.

"Well, somebody threw in the
Buddha into my life, a beautiful
young gal just at the time I really
needed it, something new. Then the Beat-
les opened me up to Maharishi and Hindu philosophy, but what it really boiled down to for
me all along, back to when I came out of Minnesota
and fell in with Joan on the anti-war efforts and
tryin' to stop the war in Vietnam, was this, for me:
it was all just an expansion into PHILOSOPHY that
worked its way into my poetry, and was never truly
about what most people call "religion."

I suggested that we go visit my friend Yolanda
since we weren't in Malibu and would have to miss
all of the fine ladies who would normally come to
his house, but when we got there to Yolanda's house
in the gentrified barrio, she was already totally
drunk, and she started throwing beer cans at my new
friend. I asked her, "Don't you know who this is?"

And she replied "I don't give a rat's ass if it
is Pancho Villa; you didn't show up with a new case
of beer!"

Dylan looked at her, broke out in a peel of laughter that might remind some people of the sound of a
hyena laughing, and just said, "I am so glad I never
wrote a song about a woman who was anything like her!"

I then woke up, and even though I knew it was all a
weird dream, I still looked around my campsite for that
Martin Dreadnought.

Stephen Fox

ARTIST/FILM PRODUCER · SANTE FE, NM

79 | UNDERGROUND ART

Large underground tunnels contain thousands of people
hoping Dylan will stage a concert. The tunnels have
been made so large that the stability of the ground
above and a housing complex nearby are under serious
threat. Dylan is there in his 1968/69 appearance, but
is somehow out of focus and elusive. It seems he does
not wish to perform. Already, books are on sale about
Dylan's visit even though he has not given a concert
yet. I pass through the broad tunnels with the huge
crowds. Outside the tunnel system I find myself as an
understudy in a play being put on at a theatre with a
famous actor (identity unknown) in the lead role. I
have my Gibson J200 guitar with me and take a seat in
the audience to watch the play.

Geoff Ward

JOURNALIST, POET, WRITER,
SINGER/SONGWRITER · IRELAND

Tuulikki Bogman

SOCIAL WORKER · STOCKHOLM, SWEDEN

85 | WITH SNAKES LIKE THESE

We were in a car. Bob was driving, then he turned into
a swamp area, and I thought he was going out to pick
flowers for me, but he left me alone there. It was
getting dark, and I was a bit nervous. Maybe there
were some snakes around. I started to feel uncomfortable alone there in the car. Then he returned, smiled
at me, and placed a bouquet of snakes at my breast.
I couldn't do anything but stay still while all those
snakes started crawling around all over me.

11

DIRECTION HOME

Pete Johnson

MUSIC DISTRIBUTOR
NEW JERSEY

Bob and I were walking somewhere in the woods. It was like walking with an old friend, but every time I asked him something he would just smile and nod.

He never spoke, but would point to different things—the dog that was with us, a tree, a bridge. Then when we got to the road, we shook hands and went home in different directions.

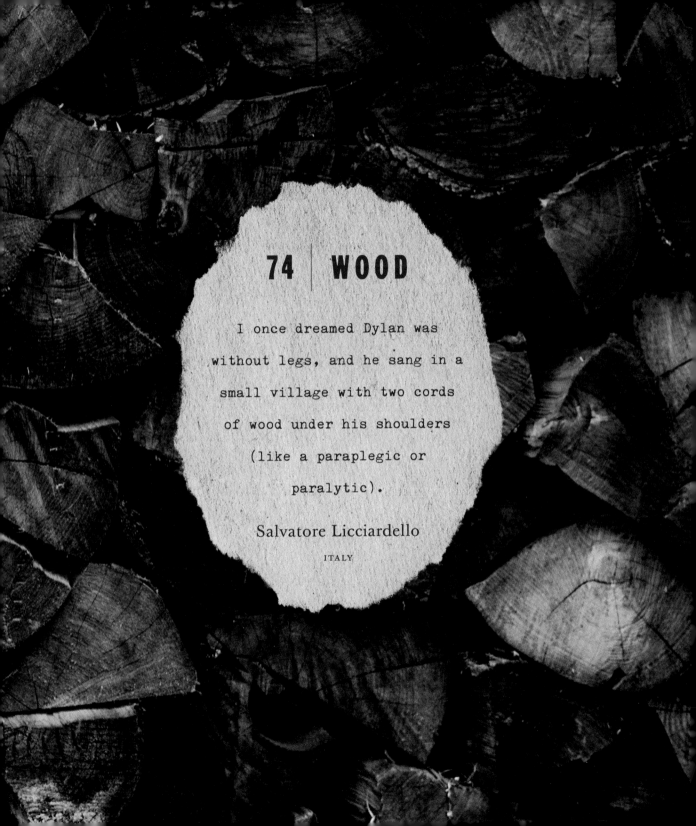

74 | WOOD

I once dreamed Dylan was
without legs, and he sang in a
small village with two cords
of wood under his shoulders
(like a paraplegic or
paralytic).

Salvatore Licciardello

ITALY

22 | UNWELCOME GUEST

I dreamed of Bob as an annoying houseguest.
He parked himself on our couch, commandeered
the remote, and sunk into that sofa. He was
wearing a hoodie—hood off—and it was clear he
wasn't going to budge. After a while, we started
dropping hints like, "Uh, Bob, do you wanna
do something else?" He just mumbled in response.
Although this was a first personal encounter
with Bob, he seemed to be an old friend,
and exasperating.

John Urda

BROOKLYN, NY

I dream that Bob and I play "Tangled Up in Blue" together, and I have

to keep reminding him what the words are.

24

CLOWNS

He is wearing a clown costume—like Bozo, but not with

such big hair. I am wearing a Nazi uniform, but a bit more

frilly than usual. Bob seems to LIKE being ordered around.

Maybe he is into being submissive. I can't tell.

On the last verse, he takes one of his big clown

shoes and throws it at my guitar. I use my Martin D18 as a baseball bat

and hit the shoe right back to him. It hits his fake nose, knocks it

off, and he begins to cry, "Woody, Woody, I miss you man."

Rob Pollack

ATTORNEY

53 | THERE, GONE

The atmosphere is electric. I'm so excited, and everyone around me is buzzing, aware that Dylan's in the building, and that alone seems enough to justify this intense excitement. Then the moment comes when the lights go down and a figure appears on stage. And although he starts singing a Bob Dylan song, he looks and sounds almost nothing like Dylan.

At this point it's very dark. After a while the lights go up, and the figure is revealed to be a middle-aged man with shabby clothes and a long and scruffy beard. He's wearing a harmonica holder, but keeps pushing it up and down during songs, hardly playing it. It seems to be in the way, whether he's playing it or not. I'm thinking to myself, "He's just warming up, he needs a couple of songs to get into it." After a couple more songs, I think maybe this is one of those nights that he's just not going to deliver, or perhaps he'll pull something out of the bag at the last minute. Then I notice half the crowd has left, and the lights have gotten very bright. The next minute, almost the entire hall is empty except for me and Bob, and he has just stopped playing. He's sitting on a cheap metal chair by the drum kit scratching his head, looking downwards.

It is only then that I realize it isn't Bob at all. On the way out of the theatre, I notice all the staff and ticket people have gone. There isn't a soul left working there. Walking down the street towards the tube I see a poster on a wall advertising "Bob Dylan In Concert."

Martin Gayfords   UNITED KINGDOM

82 | RIVER'S END

In my dream, I'm floating down a river in the Amazon.
The colors were very vivid—lush green trees pillowing
over the banks of the river, tall flowers in reds and
blues and yellows, and a clear, ocean-blue river with
fine sand below. I was floating on river tubes with my
younger brother beside me and friends a few yards up
the river. Suddenly, everyone was gone and the river
ended. As I floated, still at the edge of the river's
end, a cloud appeared in the sky above me. Dylan was
hovering over me in this cloud with his guitar strapped
around him, hanging on his back. He was dressed in black
and grey and wearing a hat. He told me, with one hand
on the neck of his guitar, and a voice unmistakably
Dylan's, "Your strength will get you through it."

Jill Mansfield
WASHINGTON

18 | DIRTY GIRL

I was in a place that seemed both outdoors and indoors at the same time. There were people everywhere, trying to escape from something—either a disease or possibly aliens that were killing everyone. I was trying to get to a show, and there were people I knew from Australia who were also performing there. Some of them had died already. I was with a friend, and somehow we knew how to escape the disease/aliens and were treading over corpses, still trying to get to the show.

Eventually we made it down to the water. It was swampy. There were some aristocratic women there, dressed up as if for a ball. They were trying to convince us to come nearer. I knew they were dangerous, so I didn't go near them. Then my friend turned into Bob Dylan. I saw him near a woman with long, dark hair who was covered in soil. She was naked and had huge breasts, and was swinging from some kind of tree, above the water, covered in soil. She looked a bit like Betty Paige. Bob Dylan laughed and called her "enormous bosom" in a foreign language I'd never heard before. I laughed too. At that point my alarm clock went off and I woke up.

Greta Gertler

SINGER/SONGWRITER · NEW YORK

78 | WHAT'S IN YOUR FREEZER?

I was in his house, maybe cleaning the kitchen, and was about to do something with the freezer. I thought there was too much ice in there and started to take some away. Then I saw he had three black puppies in there, deep-frozen.

Tuulikki Bogman

SOCIAL WORKER
STOCKHOLM, SWEDEN

62 | DUET WITH DOG

Bob Dylan is in a movie on TV. It's a silent foreign movie, and the subtitles are the lyrics to his songs, translated into a foreign language. A dog is chasing him, and then a policeman is chasing both of them. They all break for lunch, and then the chasing starts again. There's a concert at the end, and the dog joins Bob Dylan for a duet.

Morten Jonsson

FOOD TECHNOLOGIST
MICHIGAN CITY, IN

02-19-2000

39 | WISDOM

In my dream, he warned me not to work too hard. He said,
"If I would have slowed down before the motorcycle accident,
I would have still had the accident, but it would have been
a minor incident. That was funny and I thought to myself in
the dream, "How can I manage to take these words from the
clouds into my day-consciousness?" But I did.

Eva
THE NETHERLANDS

76 | FULFILLED

I had to ride with someone else to a Dylan concert and
was forced to leave before the end. Before leaving,
I asked a young man to attempt to get a message to
Bob Dylan just to see if I could. The message read
"I'll let you be in my dreams if I can be in yours."

Bob said, "Yes, you are in my dreams,"
and then I woke up.

Terri
KENTUCKY

I have a recurring dream with a few variations that Bob and I are good friends. I am always surprised when I wake up and realize that he doesn't actually know me.

We meet on the street somewhere, and Bob is usually glad to see me. Sometimes he doesn't have much time for me, like he is heading out on the road. When we do get together, we often head to a coffee shop to get caught up on things. He asks me questions about theology and the Bible (since I am theologically trained), and I instruct him on difficult or technical questions about the Bible. He is very interested in prophecy, the end of the world, and things regarding the great judgment day, as well as questions about predestination, election, and God's sovereignty over the entire world. He shares insights into human nature and poetry and folk music history with me. He tells me about Charlie Patton, Jimmie Rogers, Odetta, and other more obscure figures that I'd never heard of.

He describes things he is working on and how fed up he is with it all, and I encourage him to keep using his gifts to do his thing and not let the turkeys get him down.

Doug Fox

COMPUTER NETWORK SPECIALIST · CONNECTICUT

72 | WHITE

I am carried on the shoulders of other people.
I have on a white sarong and am wearing a crown
in a big white marble building. Behind the row
of white columns there is an open hall; the
floor is checked black and white. There are big
palm plants and a grand white piano. I am drink-
ing wine and dancing with Bob, and we are naked.
The view through the columns of this big marble
hall is a beautiful, sunny, somewhat misty land-
scape where you can see hills, valleys, trees,
and bushes for miles and miles. The dirt is
yellow, and far away there are bluish mountains.
I have a happy and loving feeling in my heart.

Pia Mariana Olterman

GOTHENBURG, SWEDEN

100 | PJs

I was on stage with Dylan, played the guitar really good
for what felt like half of a show right next to him, and
it felt so real and natural, but like most dreams they
fall apart once you become aware you are dreaming. Once
that happened I was on stage in my pajamas not knowing how
to play guitar. Dylan and the audience were all looking
at me, all pissed off. I was ruining the show.

Frank Gregorin

38 | DIG IT

I was digging a ditch with Bob
but he had no shovel.

Bill Peters

MR. TANGERINE MAN AT LEUKEN'S
VILLAGE FOODS · SAN DIEGO, CA

58 | MIDDLE WITH CLASS

I dreamed I was in the back seat of a car with Dylan and
President Obama. I was in the middle. Obama was on my left
and Dylan on my right. I wondered why we were only in a sedan
and not a limo or big SUV. The ride was swervy and bumpy, and
I realized I didn't have my seat belt on, so I started to put
it on. My leg touched Dylan's leg. I was a bit self-conscious
about it, but he didn't seem to mind so I left it there.

Ellie Foltz PAINTER · YPSILANTI, MI

I had an operation that went wrong,
and I almost died. During the time when
I was near death, I had an amazing
out-of-body experience involving Bob.

48 | MEET ME IN THE MORNING

Suddenly I'm 17, back at school on the stage
in assembly, and I'm half leaning half sitting on
a tall stool. I've got long hair. I look good.
I'm playing a wicked electric bass.

Opposite me is Bob Dylan circa 1966—
big hair, Carnaby Street suit, Cuban heels,
and black Fender. We're just starting
"Visions of Johanna":

"Ain't it just like the night
to play tricks..."

I take note of the irony,
and then we're off.
There's a powerful spotlight
above us, and it's dark outside
our circle. There's a gentle
breeze blowing, and I can sense
rather than see a big warm
generous audience all around us.
My mum, who is dead, is in
the audience, and friends
from different periods of
my life are there.

I come round a bit to a
nurse telling me not to go to
sleep and me smiling and
going back to Bob.
We start a second song and
boy, could I play!

John Kehoe

UNITED KINGDOM

65 | MONEY BACK?

Bob was playing a living room show in an old house with wide-board floors broken up into many small rooms like parlors and entranceways and sitting rooms. I was in a side room, and I could see him through one doorway, where he was sitting in a big wing chair at the front of the room. Then he moved to the back of the room, where he crouched down near that doorway, and the band was cranking, and Bob was singing down there like a wild man. I'm not sure what they were playing and never really saw any instruments or anybody in the band. It was loud and growly. I just watched him and smiled a huge, ear-to-ear, shit-eating grin, and he turned his head and looked up at me and winked. Damn! Then he took a little break and sat back down in the big chair. The house was full of people, but nobody approached him. They were getting antsy for more show, but Bob had fallen asleep sitting up in the big chair. I could see he was slouched a little and his eyes were closed. Next thing I know, the band had carried him out saying that the show was cut short because somebody had let Bob get into the good vodka. I have a feeling it was me.

I went into the room where he had been and the people were all just sitting or standing around, maybe getting their coats on, grumbling and muttering. One big grey-haired, balding pale guy who was wearing a blue button-down shirt and sitting in a chair that was turned away from the corner where Bob had been sitting looked up at me and asked, "Are we going to get a refund?"

*name withheld

2 | END TIMES

Dylan was giving a concert on/in an Incan pyramid that was also part of the Wisconsin Dells and wearing a headband that was also a wig. It also happened to be the end of the world. I'd been burned by napalm, which healed as soon as I got to where his concert was. He was playing with a Mariachi band. Halfway through the concert, he decided to go through some local menus to figure out what he wanted for dinner. Then he jumped off stage and spent the rest of the time taking pictures of the audience.

M. C. Israel

UNIVERSITY OF MICHIGAN

37 | PICTURE THIS

Dylan had just used his natural aggressiveness and rebellion to become a force, but it was not New York City in the early '60s. Dylan was subject to mass attention and had enormous influence. Following my natural impulses, I became like him, but as myself—a larger-than-life, aesthetically interesting prototype of myself.

We were immediately pursued by reporters and crowds. We dived into an avant-garde restaurant and, as people looked for us, hid in a picture frame on the wall. Dylan and I moved in the frame, but no one noticed. Sometimes I was on the floor watching the two of us moving in the frame. Dylan had long black hair, like Richard Bach's description of Donald Shimoda.

David Sallach

SOCIAL SCIENTIST · CHICAGO, IL

49 | HANK № 2

I have casual conversations
with Bob in my dreams about
family, movies we've seen,
and sometimes we are
playing guitars in his
barn/living room, singing
Hank Williams songs.

Kevin Odegard

BLOOD ON THE TRACKS GUITARIST

95 | GIRL, WOMAN

Riding down an escalator in a large
department store (Harrod's?), I hear Bob Dylan
behind me. I turn around, and it's a small girl about
ten years old doing a phenomenal imitation. I ask her
to sing "Just Like a Woman" because I want to get this
on video. She refuses, saying that's a silly song. I turn
around, embarrassed, and try to think of a better song
to ask for. I decide maybe "Blowin' in the Wind"
or "Talkin' World War III Blues." Really not silly.
I turn back around, and either she's suddenly
turned into a woman or it's someone else.
I'm so confused I wake up.

Sander Anderson

ATTORNEY · LONDON

114 | FRISSON

In my dreams, Bob is always super friendly and psyched to hang out with me. Usually we're making plans to collaborate on some Big Project that's very secretive. NO ONE must know. That's the fun bit...bein' all sneaky together.

I discover that Bob is playing a show in my neck of the woods. Miraculously, I'm able to cut through all the security and end up in close proximity to him. We exchange furtive glances across a wood-paneled room. Immediately, he recognizes me: a sexy, spirited, like-minded soul. Mona Lisa smiles are exchanged. There is no hero worship, only mutual respect—okay, and a certain "frisson."

We make a subtle head-nod and escape the crowd for somewhere quiet. It's dark. Red velvet is involved. We speak in whispered tones. We conspire. We laugh. We nuzzle...and then...and then...

I wake up. Damn.

Alex Forbes

SONGWRITER, SONGWRITING COACH

44 | IF ONLY

I used to have a recurring dream of finding myself in the record department of Alexander's Department Store and seeing 40 or 50 Dylan albums on display that I didn't know about. It was paradise flipping through them. Needless to say, it was a dream from which I did not wish to awaken.

Jim Steinblatt

MUSIC WRITER · NEW YORK, NY

35 | HE ONLY SWEARS IN MY DREAMS

In 2002 or 2003, I dreamed I was Bob's drummer, complete with
period-correct fellow band members. We had an outdoor show
in some small town in the middle of nowhere, probably in the
Mountain Time Zone, craggy hills on one side, two-lane
highway on the other. There was a tent, somewhat haphazardly
erected, where the show was to be. The entire organization of
the show was deemed to be inept; disorganization was the only
organization. The paying audience was exceedingly small.
It was overcast and very windy; I think a storm threatened.

When Bob emerged from his bus to survey the motley scene,
he immediately said, "I'm not playing this fucking show,"
got back on his bus, and the bus departed. The rest of us,
band and crew and promoter and audience, were left scratching
our heads. My last thought in the dream was, "Now I'll
never get to play drums with Bob Dylan!"

Will Rigby

DRUMMER · DURHAM, NC

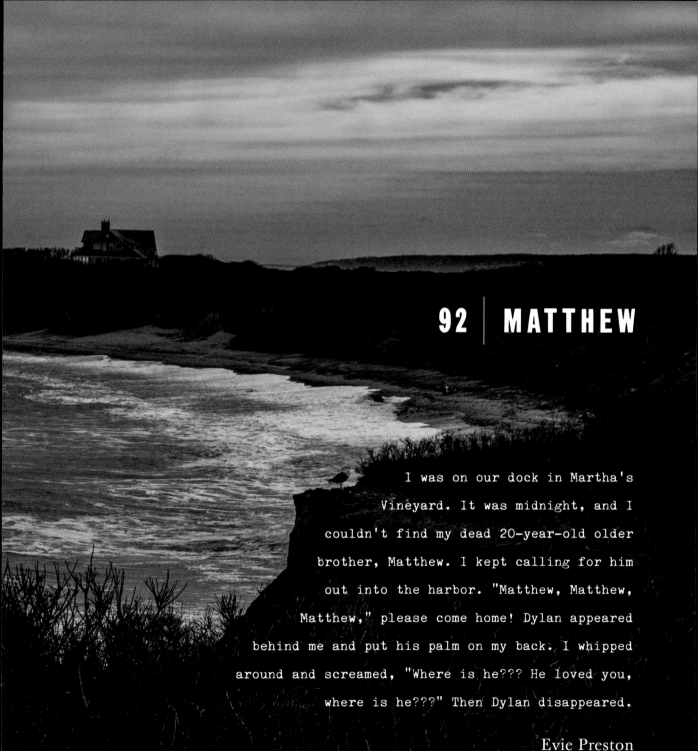

92 | MATTHEW

I was on our dock in Martha's Vineyard. It was midnight, and I couldn't find my dead 20-year-old older brother, Matthew. I kept calling for him out into the harbor. "Matthew, Matthew, Matthew," please come home! Dylan appeared behind me and put his palm on my back. I whipped around and screamed, "Where is he??? He loved you, where is he???" Then Dylan disappeared.

Evie Preston

I was on the phone with Bob's manager who said,

"You want to talk to Bob? Who is this?"

I said, "Trish."

Bob got on the phone
and said,

"Hi China.
Have you ever had
any kids?"

I was trying
to explain that I
told the guy
my name was Trish,
and I
couldn't hear what
Bob was saying and
I woke up.

88 | T-R-I-S-H

Trish Rodenbaugh

POST OFFICE · NEW JERSEY

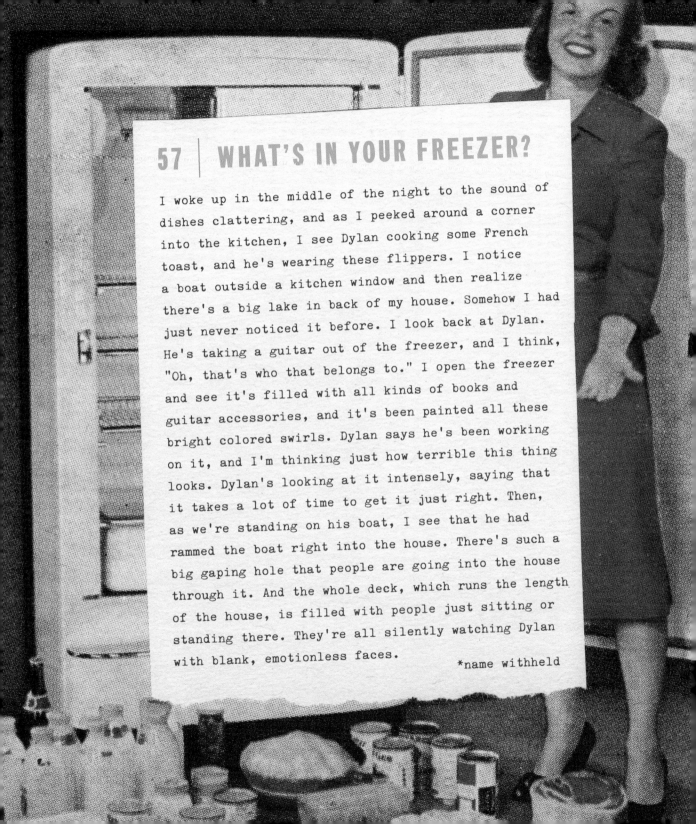

I woke up in the middle of the night to the sound of dishes clattering, and as I peeked around a corner into the kitchen, I see Dylan cooking some French toast, and he's wearing these flippers. I notice a boat outside a kitchen window and then realize there's a big lake in back of my house. Somehow I had just never noticed it before. I look back at Dylan. He's taking a guitar out of the freezer, and I think, "Oh, that's who that belongs to." I open the freezer and see it's filled with all kinds of books and guitar accessories, and it's been painted all these bright colored swirls. Dylan says he's been working on it, and I'm thinking just how terrible this thing looks. Dylan's looking at it intensely, saying that it takes a lot of time to get it just right. Then, as we're standing on his boat, I see that he had rammed the boat right into the house. There's such a big gaping hole that people are going into the house through it. And the whole deck, which runs the length of the house, is filled with people just sitting or standing there. They're all silently watching Dylan with blank, emotionless faces.

*name withheld

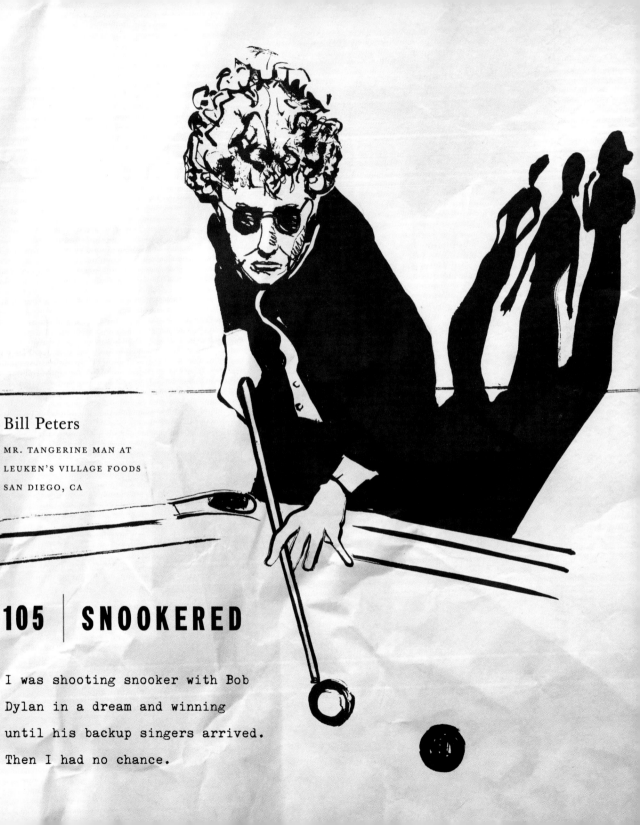

Bill Peters

MR. TANGERINE MAN AT
LEUKEN'S VILLAGE FOODS
SAN DIEGO, CA

105 | SNOOKERED

I was shooting snooker with Bob
Dylan in a dream and winning
until his backup singers arrived.
Then I had no chance.

40 | L'IL BUDDY

I'm on the NET tour with Bob, and we're
hanging out, best of pals, as we go from town
to town. I'm so much part of his inner circle that
he has a special nickname for me: L'il Buddy. This is
quite funny since I'm 220 pounds, 6 feet tall, and
towering over Bob. Basically, Bob won't shut up:
"Where do we eat, L'il Buddy?" "Wanna shoot some pool,
L'il Buddy?" "What are we doin' after the show,
L'il Buddy?" Every time Bob asks me something
I crack up laughing, probably because I should
be calling him L'il Buddy, not vice versa.

Peter Dare

ADVERTISING EXECUTIVE/EDUCATIONAL
CONSULTANT · QUEBEC

83 | THE LEDGE

Patty Forbes

PSYCHOTHERAPIST · NEW YORK, NY

He carried me over a high ledge. I closed my eyes and gripped his neck tightly, but trusted him because he's, well, he's him! It was very risky and seemed dangerous. I was surprised that he would be so reckless as to take a chance like that. But he's, well, he's him.

101 | DON'T LET ME DOWN

Sarah Post   NEW HAVEN, CT

I am with a touring band, just off the bus outside a country house somewhere overlooking a lake. Feels like late fall. Everything is a faded
brown. For some reason, we are all perched on the ledge of a steep cliff
just outside the house. Dylan is crouched to my left. His face is very
young, soft, and smooth. I feel that I am slipping off the ledge, which
would be death. I ask if someone can pull me back. Dylan says, "No."

66 | HOME

I was in my parents' kitchen in Chicago, chopping up vegetables for salad. Bob was in the kitchen with me. We were talking comfortably, old friends, when it suddenly struck me, "Omigawd, I'm having a long personal conversation with Bob Dylan!" I put down my knife and stared at him. He stopped talking, and we stared at each other, smiling. I was trying to make sure it was real, that I wasn't dreaming, and the more we stared at each other, the more real it became to me. There was nothing star-struck about it or weird at all. We were just really good close friends. He knew what was going on in my head and nodded his. We both suddenly broke out into long loud laughter. I was so happy. Of course, when I woke up I was very sad. Some dreams you wish would never end.

Elena Skye

SINGER/SONGWRITER
HOBOKEN, NJ

I was in an old tavern with Bob Dylan and Charles Bukowski.
I walked in between them up to the bar and ordered a Coca-
Cola (this dream occurred about two months into my becoming
sober after years of alcoholism). Bukowski asked Dylan, "Ya
think he's gonna make it?" Dylan responded, "He might be a
true rebel, rebelling against rebellion." Then Dylan walked
up to a small stage, sat on a stool, and began strumming
the guitar. Bukowski stunk of beer and told me, "He is gonna
play this one for you." I couldn't at all make out what he
was playing or singing. It sounded Dylanesque but muffled,
like a bad bootleg, complete with annoying crowd noises,
hoots, and hollers. I was disappointed and went back to the
bar and ordered a cocktail. Before it arrived, I looked up,
and Dylan was gone. I got up and left the bar in terror.
Woke up. Twelve years later, I haven't had a drink.

*name withheld

54 | HOMEWRECKER

I am walking in Central Park, and I see him. He's wearing
shades, but somehow we make eye contact and smile, and then
we're together. Like we followed a clear impulse. Next thing
I remember is that we're sitting next to each other at a long
table somewhere, and it's as though we're having an affair
or are talking about having an affair. We're doing something
together at the table, maybe writing in a book. It's like a
reception table at an event where you might look for your
nametag. We're inserting little cards into slots on the pages
of the book. My real-life husband is off in the distance
wearing a white suit. I tell Bob that my husband always knows
everything. He is very smart and will definitely figure out
that we're together. Then my husband comes by the table and
asks where I've been; I was supposed to be somewhere and
wasn't. I make something up, and I'm talking to him like he's
a stranger, coldly. I was bonded to Bob and not to him.

Susan Welchire

NEUROLOGIST · CHICAGO, IL

84 | PFSD

It was a young, shorter-haired, New York City
Dylan. A "Positively Fourth Street" Dylan. In the
dream, I was in the middle of some kind of vague,
not good situation, and there he was, crooking/
tilting his head and smiling at me. I think we
knew each other, and we just start dancing—not
hippy, groovy dancing but old school, slow,
sweet, and close. A really nice comforting dream.

Viva HC

69 | TOYING

Here he was again, standing in my doorway. Lithe, almost young, leathery skin and twinkling blue eyes and that old granddad shirt from the <u>Blood</u> <u>on</u> <u>the</u> <u>Tracks</u> years. The paradox was not lost in the dream. Me, a 48-year-old fumbling sometime musician, and the maestro, at this point in time at least 20 years my junior. He oozed charm as he sat in the living room chatting and joking with my family. Was that Joan on the piano in the corner or my younger sister? I could not confirm. Bob had already thrust an Epiphone semi-acoustic bass into my hand with the instruction to learn the chords

for the next gig. The Epiphone was my first guitar as
a college student 30 years ago. I had sold it after I
realized I could never manage to master the roots to the
chords and keep in time! But Bob trusted me with it.

"Bob, can I play my acoustic?" I knew I would feel more
comfortable.

He walked across the hall and into the dining room,
where I was standing. Behind him came my mother, father,
and children. He handed me a tiny red Stratocaster,
with buttons instead of strings. I took it, and it immediately began screaming out the opening riffs of "All
Along the Watchtower." The guitar was a toy. Bob wasn't
impressed, but he smiled all the same.

Nic Outterside

WRITER · UNITED KINGDOM

32 | IF YOU GOTTA GO (№ 1)

I am in a living room where there is a mother dog and her puppy.
The mother is trying to housetrain the puppy. Dylan is standing
in between the kitchen and living room on a wall-mounted phone,
à la the '70s. He is housetraining another dog. Both of these
dogs have to go to the bathroom, but are being made to stay
inside for a while. Dylan and the mother are on the same page
about this. I am sitting on the living room sofa watching it
all, having to go the bathroom myself.

Veronica Rain

SINGER/SONGWRITER · DETROIT, MI

33 | IF YOU GOTTA GO (№ 2)

The radiator is knocking in the bathroom. It's the radiator from
my apartment in college. I thought I'd never have to hear it
again, now that I have central air. The knocking means I have to
finish my history term paper tonight. And it has to be in Span-
ish. I'm scared the noise will upset my dog and he'll pee on
the bathmat. I can't have Bob Dylan stepping on my pee-soaked
bathmat. Bob Dylan tilts his head, listening to the knocking. I
listen too, trying to hear the way Bob Dylan hears, to attune
myself to the rhythm in his head. He scratches his chest between
the buttons of his shirt. "¿Dónde está el baño?" he says.

Morten Jonsson

FOOD TECHNOLOGIST · MICHIGAN CITY, IN

47 | NOVA

Throughout high school, as now, I was fanatic about Dylan and the Stones. In my senior year at White Plains High School, I drove a car my parents had gotten for my use and my older brother's use, too. A cranberry Nova Super Sport 350 engine. Fast as a rabbit.

My older brother hated the fact that I also used the car at the stable where I kept a horse because it always smelled of horses when he wanted to use it for his "dates." I barely noticed the smell myself, so I never really cleaned it up.

One night, my short dream was that I had the car in the driveway at high school near the athletic fields. I was sitting in the "offending trunk" with the hood open of course, and sitting with me were Bob Dylan and Keith Richards, our derrieres in the trunk, our legs dangling out over the back of the car. We had shades on, and we were just hangin'. Evidently, the horse smell didn't bother them at all, which I took as approval of my earth-loving nature.

When I woke up, all I wanted to do was go back to the trunk of that car and hang with my heroes...but you know how that goes.

Meg Griffin   SIRIUS XM DJ

98 | ROUGH EDGES

I dreamed his voice was terrible, just a weird reptilian croak,
and then the mic cut out, and he was miming. Then there was silence,
and he just stared into the distance.

Craig Beaumont

CONSULTANT · NEW YORK, NY

102 | STOREFRONT

I had a Dylan-related dream long ago, maybe
around 1971. The tap-tap-tapping of the drums
on "Sad-Eyed Lady of the Lowlands" was the
musical backdrop as I was walking down a street
with several storefronts. I stopped at one,
a pawnshop, and peered through the window.
Inside, I saw all sorts of magical and mystical
things, while the tap-tap-tapping continued.
It was beautiful dream, indeed.

George Spanos

FORMER EDUCATOR · ARLINGTON, VA

93 | FATHER FIGURE

When Bob Dylan has appeared in my dreams, as he has
many times over the years, it is always in some
variation of this scenario: we are playing music
together, either informally (in a dressing room,
or in someone's home) or on an actual gig in which I am in his backing
band. Invariably, he is initially skeptical of my musical vocabulary,
but I eventually manage to win him over by surprising him with obscu-
rities (mostly old country or really early pop tunes), leading to a
sense of camaraderie and good feeling between us—clearly a take on the
son trying to prove himself to the father, which makes sense given that
Dylan played that role for me during my formative years as a musician
and performer.

Howard Fishman

WRITER, COMPOSER, PERFORMER · BROOKLYN, NY

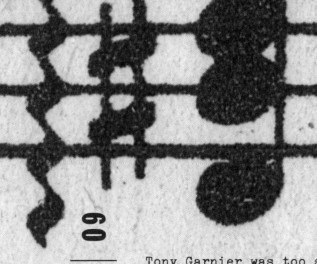

60 | SUB BASE

Tony Garnier was too sick to play and would be out of commission for at least a week, maybe more. So Bob was looking for a replacement. I was backstage somehow, and Dylan's manager said that Bob had asked him if I could fill in until Tony got better. I caught a glimpse of Bob as he walked away from me and out the door going towards the stage, strapping on a white Fender Stratocaster as he went. He had on a white dress shirt, unbuttoned at the top, with suspenders and black slacks. He was calm and seemed very down-to-earth, ready to go to work. He didn't speak directly to me, but I had the distinct impression he felt very confident in my ability to carry my weight playing bass. His confidence was catching, and I felt gratified and looked forward to enjoying the evening and days ahead.

Andy Weiskoff · ATLANTA, GA

28 | TWINS

I was opening for Dylan, and somehow I ended up in a hotel room with him and his manager. There were two twin beds. He and the manager were lying in one bed. I was in the other. It was a nondescript, off-white room. The manager went out to get some soda or something to bring back to the room. So Bob and I were alone. At one point we looked at each other and started giggling about the fact that here we were alone together "in bed." We sat up and faced each other, still sitting on our separate beds with our knees touching and we held hands, giggling and enjoying each other. It was as though we'd been wanting to do this and now, at last with the grownups gone, we were free.

He made some comment along the lines of, "You haven't seen anyone getting photos of me, or helped anyone get information

about me?" I told him I hadn't. Then we lay together in my
bed. I was thinking about how great it is when it's new and
there's that tingly feeling. And the fear. I thought about how
I would/should withdraw because I was married. I fantasized
about telling him about what a good guy my husband was. I said
something like, "Maybe I should be the one to worry about
hidden cameras." I felt very comfortable. We were very happy
being together.

   The manager came back, and we went back to the separate beds.
Bob was bitching that the manager hadn't gotten the right
stuff. I was stepping over luggage on the floor—a big white
hard-shelled suitcase. Bob and I were feeling very together.
Then I went into this other room and saw a huge office. I said
I didn't know there was an office there and joked that maybe
I'd do some work. "Maybe I'll invent something," I said.

                    *name withheld

99 | FRIENDS

I had a dream that it was 1987, Dylan and I
were friends, and we were hanging out on a lake.
He had on leather gloves with no fingers.
We were on a dock, fishing, and he wanted to
take the boat out to fish on the lake. I was kind
of arguing with him. I knew I could disagree with
him because we were friends, in my dream.

Dylan Gikas

ENVIRONMENTAL CONSULTANT · MINNESOTA

94 | STOP

Two summers ago, I was in New Jersey with some
friends for a few days. We got stuck in a ton
of evening traffic on the way back to Brooklyn.
There was Bob Dylan music playing in the car, and
for some reason it was annoying me. Usually,
I very much enjoy his music, but that evening I
had a dream that I was telling Bob to just stop.
Just stop it already. Not sure if it was stop
singing or just telling him to stop something.
The only thing that really stopped was the dream.

Stacey Luckow

STORE OWNER, THE 9TH STREET HABERDASHERY
NEW YORK, NY

68 | SOUL TO SOUL

In the dream, Dylan is 64, and I somehow found him
after much searching. Yet, he knew already that we were
supposed to meet, and he was not surprised to see me. He received
me warmly, and we sat and talked for hours. We talked in that
soul-quenchingly deep way where you lose all sense of time and place
and delve into matters that seem to nourish the soul just in talking
about them. We connected so completely, and it was such a profound
experience that it just seemed destined to happen. We spoke of everything:
life, death, love, society, music, poetry, pain, joy, the mind.
I asked him everything I had ever wanted to know about him and his
incredible mind and music, and he gladly divulged all information
because he knew that there was an underlying reason for our meeting.
He knew that it was right. I woke up in the middle of the night
feeling as if I had been through a spiritual experience.
Do you think it's possible that souls travel during
sleep? Maybe Dylan's soul and mine did meet
that night. You never know.

Kelly

29 | MY 115 DREAMS OF
BOB DYLAN

My recurring dreams of Bob Dylan lasted for about twelve years and
always took place in my friend Anna's 1970s-style kitchen, sitting
at her table having conversations with Bob Dylan.

* * *

At first, my dreams of Dylan were a recounting of my previous
day's activities. In the first couple of years when I was still
close to Anna, I would sit and have what seemed like a normal
two-way conversation with Bob about what was going on in my life:
girlfriends, jobs, conflicts, what I was reading, what I was listening to, what I was writing. It seemed like a useful tool to sit
down and talk to my favorite artist every night about the events
of the previous day; he was always a gracious conversationalist
and always encouraging to me about whatever I was reading and

especially encouraging about my writing. But as I got older and moved away from my hometown, the dreams became less frequent, and it seemed my Dylan dreams only came to me over the next decade during times of great conflict in my life. Then I would sit and recount the times of my life with him, and he began to answer me more like a professional therapist. He would say things like "Uh huh," "Go on, tell me more," "How did that make you feel?" "What did you do about that?" But it always seemed like the most important, most therapeutic thing he would say was, "Have you written anything about it?" or "You should write something about that," or "Let's talk again after you written something about it." I cannot say how much his constant advice to write something about the times of conflict in my life have helped me; it certainly helped make me a person who writes often and honestly about—as Warren Zevon would say—"my dirty life and times."

Lawrence Simon

MICHIGAN STATE DEPT. OF CORRECTIONS (RET.) · CLARKLAKE, MI

30 | **PRISONERS**

M. Willbury

I dreamed Dylan and John Lennon were being chased across rooftops and shot at by a SWAT team.

55 | NEIGHBORS

I'm in the top floor apartment of a building in Manhattan. It's very dark and dingy, despite the windows, and nearly unfurnished, with wide-plank wooden floors. There's a table at one end facing the windows. Suddenly Dylan walks through. He'd been on the roof and was passing through my apartment to get to the hallway. He's wearing a black velour running suit. Apparently, he has a small, equally dingy apartment on the same floor. It feels surprising to me that he would want such a thing, but he seems very happy with this arrangement. He walks past me, smiles and says, "Hi, Mary Lee," leaving me flattered and happy that he knows me.

Mary Lee Kortes

MUSICIAN, AUTHOR · BROOKLYN, NY

ABOUT THE AUTHOR

Mary Lee Kortes is a musician and author based in Brooklyn, New York. She has released five albums of original material to wide critical acclaim, each of which landed on the Billboard critics' top ten list in the year of its debut. Rolling Stone described her voice as "the high-mountain sunshine of Dolly Parton, with a sweet-iron under-coat of Chrissie Hynde." In 2002, Mary Lee released a song-for-song recording of Bob Dylan's classic Blood on the Tracks LP. She has toured the world both as a headliner and an opening act for established artists, including Dylan. Kortes is also a published short story writer. Dreaming of Dylan: 115 Dreams About Bob is her first book.

ART CREDITS

Title page spread: Photograph by Daniel Root

Foreword (Dylan figure): Illustration by Rina Root

Dream 106 (left-hand page): Photograph by Daniel Root; snow globe contains a photograph by Daniel Kramer

Dream 104: Illustration by Kevin Walters

Dream 103: Photograph by Daniel Root

Dream 75: Photograph by Barry Feinstein

Dream 3: Photograph by Daniel Root

Dream 67: Photograph by Daniel Root

Dream 9: Illustration by Kevin Walters

Dream 12 & 5: Photograph by Daniel Root

Dream 31: Photograph by Daniel Root

Dream 61: Photograph by Daniel Root

Dream 10: Illustration by Kevin Walters

Dream 27: Photographs by Daniel Root

Dream 81: Photograph by Daniel Root

Dream 113: Photograph by Daniel Root

Dream 79: Illustration by Kevin Walters

Dream 77 (right-hand page): Photograph by Daniel Root

Dream 71: Illustration by Rina Root

Dream 1: Illustration by Jenny Laden

Dream 20: Photograph by Daniel Root

Dream 14 (left-hand page): Photograph by Daniel Root

Dream 21: Photograph by Daniel Root

Dream 4: Illustration by Gene Goodale

Dream 109: Photograph by Daniel Root

Dream 19: Painting by Jerry Pagane

Dream 89 & 45: Photograph by Daniel Root

Dream 80, 111 & 56: Photograph by Barry Feinstein

Dream 25 (Dylan eyes fragment): original photo by Daniel Kramer, scanned from Star Time magazine, Oct 1966

Dream 13: Illustration by Kevin Walters

Dream 11: Illustration by Rina Root

Dream 74: Photograph by Daniel Root

Dream 53: Photograph by Barry Feinstein

Dream 78 & 62: Photograph by Daniel Root

Dream 39 & 76: Illustration by Stanley Mouse

Dream 58: Illustration by Jenny Laden

Dream 65: Illustration by Rina Root

Dream 2: Illustration by Kevin Walters

Dream 95: Painting ("Tangled Up in Blue") by Stanley Mouse

Dream 35 & 92: Photograph by Daniel Root

Dream 105: Illustration by Rina Root

Dream 32 & 33 (left-hand page): Photograph by Daniel Root

Dream 47: Illustration by Kevin Walters

Dream 102 (right-hand page): Photograph by Daniel Root

Dream 68 (right-hand page): Photograph by Daniel Root

Dream 30: Illustration by Kevin Walters

Author photograph: Michael Inglesh

All other artwork comprised of stock imagery and assorted 20th century print ephemera

ACKNOWLEDGMENTS

My life is populated with smart, gifted, generous people, and so there are
many to thank for helping me bring this book to life. Of the many, I'd
first like to thank my publishers, Scott B. Bomar and Kate Hyman of BMG
Books, who saw something viable in this wacky idea and jumped on board with
enthusiasm and support at every turn. Thank you, Kate, for your invaluable
creativity, dedication, and belief. And Scott, thank you for making this
dream come true.

To my agent Kevin O'Connor of the O'Connor Literary Agency: Thank you for
taking me on, for your unfailing guidance, commitment to excellence, and
for always knowing what to do!

Another very special thanks goes to Mitch Blank, who's been archiving all
things Dylan for decades and is now Associate Archivist at the Bob Dylan
Archive, based in Tulsa. Mitch is, quite simply, a great soul. He opened
his doors and vast knowledge to me during my <u>Blood</u> <u>on</u> <u>the</u> <u>Tracks</u> days and
then again for this book, letting us photograph anything and everything
we wanted, understanding what I was going for, offering suggestions and
direction. Photographs of his wild archive comprise a large part of the
beauty and abundance in these pages. Mitch, I can't thank you enough.

Speaking of photographs: Thank you to photographer/artist Daniel Root for
your stunning and inventive images, not only of Mitch Blank's collection,
but also for your hunts into the hidden corners of New York City at all
hours to find and photograph an image that matched a specific dream, and
then another and another.

Chris Bryson has been a supporter of this project since its early days, introducing me to the brilliant Rina Root—whose illustrations grace the cover of this book and many pages herein—and designing images to use in social media and elsewhere in my quest for dreams. Oh, and there's the countless posters and gig flyers he's designed for me and so many musicians. Thank you, thank you, thank you, Chris.

In addition to their artistry, special mention should also be given to Daniel Root and Rina Root for their extreme generosity and commitment to helping make this project as beautiful, intriguing, and complete as possible. Thank you, Dan and Rina.

I have friends at radio who used time on their shows to announce the project and help me collect dreams. Thank you, Mojo Nixon, "The Loon in the Afternoon" on Sirius XM Radio. Your listeners had some truly loony dreams! And thank you, Mary Lamont, for spreading the word on your show "Down Home Country" on WUSB.

A million thanks to designer Mark Melnick—who understood the vision in my head better than I did—for this phenomenal book design.

For general and specific encouragement, enthusiasm, and support, I have an embarrassment of riches in friends and colleagues. Thank you to Judith Akullian, Will Blythe, Elaine Caswell, Neal Coomer, Bob Epstein, Patty Forbes, Jill Gould, Jim Keller, Maz Kessler, Laurel Lindahl, Jim Marchese, Mike Maska, Gillian McCain, Rick Moody, Katy Munger, Anne Nelson, Shelly Peiken, Julie Pewitt, Linda Plotnicki, Cathy Saypol, Ronny Schiff, Kerry Smith, and Alice Sorensen.

Profound thanks to Jeff Rosen and Special Rider Music for their generous support, both for my endeavors over the years and for this book.

To the smartest person I know, Eric Ambel: Besides everything else, thank you for the tremendous idea of photographer Daniel Root and illustrator Kevin Walters.

To the Dreamers who were brave enough to share their dreams, making their private thoughts public, thank you again and again, and then some more.

And, of course, thank you, Bob Dylan.

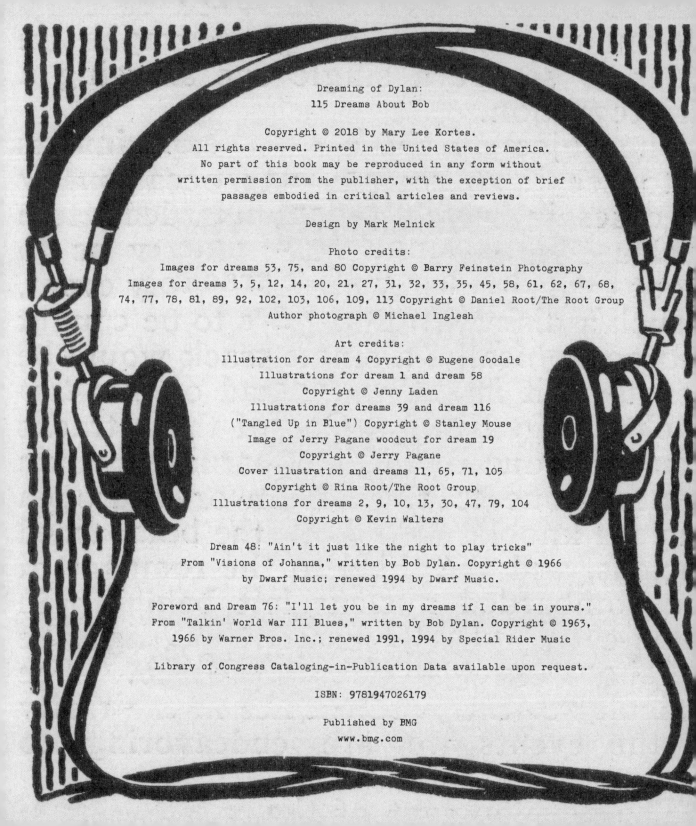

Dreaming of Dylan:
115 Dreams About Bob

Design by Mark Melnick

Photo credits:
Images for dreams 53, 75, and 80 Copyright © Barry Feinstein Photography
Images for dreams 3, 5, 12, 14, 20, 21, 27, 31, 32, 33, 35, 45, 58, 61, 62, 67, 68,
74, 77, 78, 81, 89, 92, 102, 103, 106, 109, 113 Copyright © Daniel Root/The Root Group
Author photograph © Michael Inglesh

Art credits:
Illustration for dream 4 Copyright © Eugene Goodale
Illustrations for dream 1 and dream 58
Copyright © Jenny Laden
Illustrations for dreams 39 and dream 116
("Tangled Up in Blue") Copyright © Stanley Mouse
Image of Jerry Pagane woodcut for dream 19
Copyright © Jerry Pagane
Cover illustration and dreams 11, 65, 71, 105
Copyright © Rina Root/The Root Group
Illustrations for dreams 2, 9, 10, 13, 30, 47, 79, 104
Copyright © Kevin Walters

Dream 48: "Ain't it just like the night to play tricks"
From "Visions of Johanna," written by Bob Dylan. Copyright © 1966
by Dwarf Music; renewed 1994 by Dwarf Music.

Foreword and Dream 76: "I'll let you be in my dreams if I can be in yours."
From "Talkin' World War III Blues," written by Bob Dylan. Copyright © 1963,
1966 by Warner Bros. Inc.; renewed 1991, 1994 by Special Rider Music

Library of Congress Cataloging-in-Publication Data available upon request.

ISBN: 9781947026179

Published by BMG
www.bmg.com